# The Reclamation

*Understanding and Healing the Many Wounds of Abandonment*

**Ingrid Fullerton**

**NJ Learning for All, LLC**

**The Day the Phone Rang**

For most of his life, he believed he did not need a father.

Not because he didn't know one existed. He knew there was a man somewhere in the world who shared his blood. But the subject lived in a quiet corner of his life, one he learned not to touch.

He grew up with a mother who carried the full weight of raising him. She was provider, protector, and constant presence. In his mind, she was enough.

Questions about his father existed, but they remained unspoken. Something inside him felt that asking about the man would somehow be a betrayal to the woman who had given him everything. It felt disrespectful, even disloyal.

So he told himself he did not need a father.

Independence became his quiet badge of honor. He learned to rely on himself, to navigate life without expecting guidance from a man who had never appeared in the picture. Over time, the belief hardened into something that felt like truth.

Years passed, and eventually he built a life of his own. He became a husband, a father, and the head of his own household.

Then one day, curiosity led him somewhere unexpected.

His daughter convinced him to take a DNA test to learn more about his ancestry and discover what percentage of different regions made up his heritage. At the time, the decision felt harmless, almost casual.

He had no idea he was opening a door.

When the results returned, they revealed more than ancestry.

They revealed family.

A father.

Siblings.

An entire set of relationships he had never known existed.

The information sat on the screen in front of him undeniable. A life he had never been part of was suddenly visible.

Then an email arrived.

It was from a man ten years younger than him whose DNA results showed a close match. The message was simple but life-altering.

According to the test, they were brothers.

The realization flooded him with emotions he had never experienced before. Curiosity collided with disbelief. Questions he had never allowed himself to ask suddenly rushed forward all at once.

And then, not long after, the phone rang.

When he answered, the voice on the other end paused before speaking, as if gathering courage that had taken years to find.

The man said the words plainly.

"I am your father."

For a moment, everything inside him froze.

The sentence echoed through years of silence he had carefully learned to live with. The identity he had constructed, the one that insisted he did not need a father, suddenly felt unsettled.

Emotions surfaced quickly and without order.

Confusion.

Curiosity.

And beneath it all, something deeper recognition.

The day his father reached out was the day he realized something he had never allowed himself to admit.

He had always needed him.

Speaking with the man whose absence had shaped so much ( his life stirred emotions he had never experienced before. Pa and present collided in ways he had never prepared for.

Standing at the edge of a relationship that had never existed before, he faced a question he never imagined asking.

For years he believed he could live without his father.

But now that he had found him, the gate of confusion sudder unleashed it's power.

This book explores the many forms abandonment can take ar the quiet ways it can shape identity

Sometimes the stories we tell ourselves in order to survive are not the full truth.

Sometimes they are only the beginning of a much larger one.

## COPYRIGHT PAGE

Copyright © 2026
NJ Learning For All, LLC

Published by
NJ Learning for All, LLC

Printed in the United States of America

ISBN: 979-8-9930033-6-8

NJLearningforall@gmail.com

**This book was previously published under the title *The Heartbreak*. The content remains substantially the same.**

# TABLE OF CONTENTS

# Chapter 1

## When Love Is Taught in Different Languages
*And there is no Translator*

Most parents raised their children the only way they knew, and it is usually by providing.

They worked long hours.
They paid the bills.
They made sure there was food on the table and clothes on their children's backs.

In their minds, this was love.
It was how love had been modeled to them. It was how care had always been shown.

They were not taught to talk about feelings.
They were not taught to ask, "How did that make you feel?"
They were not taught that emotional closeness mattered as much as physical presence.

Love, to them, meant responsibility.
It meant endurance.
It meant doing what had to be done even if it cost them emotionally.

But children today are being raised in a different emotional world.

From an early age, they are taught to name their feelings.
They learn to recognize sadness, fear, and disappointment.
They are encouraged to talk, to express, to process.

They are taught that being heard matters, that emotions are valid, that connection is built through presence.

To them, love looks like conversation.
It looks like attention.
It looks like reassurance, warmth, and emotional availability

So they grow up expecting that same language at home.

And when they don't receive it, they don't think, My parent loves me in a different way.

They think,
My parent doesn't care.

That is where the disconnect begins.

Many parents are exhausted working two jobs, carrying the weight of responsibility, doing everything they can to give their children more than they had. In their minds, providing is proof of love.

But their children are not asking for more things.

They are asking for time.
For conversation.
For emotional presence.

They want to be listened to.
They want their fears acknowledged. They want to feel seen.

And when that doesn't happen, they don't protest. They internalize.

They begin to believe their feelings are inconvenient.
That they are asking for too much.
That love must be earned through silence, obedience, or independence.

What parents often don't realize is that their children are not rejecting their love.

They simply do not recognize it.

Because love is being spoken in one language and is received in another.

It is as if the parents are speaking Chinese and their children are speaking Spanish. Both are communicating. Both are sincere. Both believe they are being clear.

But without translation, meaning is lost.

The parent says, "I am working hard for you."
The child hears, "You don't have time for me."

The parent says, "Be strong."
The child hears, "Your feelings doesn't matter."

The parent says, "You'll be fine." The child hears, "You're alone with this."

No one is lying.
No one is trying to hurt the other.
But without translation, love becomes misinterpreted.

That is where emotional distance forms not through neglect or cruelty, but through misunderstanding.

This book exists to be that translator.

It is written for the adult child who grew up feeling unseen, confused by their emotions, or guilty for wanting more than what was given.

And it is written for the parent who loved deeply, sacrificed endlessly, and never realized their child needed a different expression of that love and for parents who find themselves estranged from their adult children and are searching for understanding. This book invites parents to gently explore that possibility, not with blame, but with compassion and clarity. Because love was always there.

It just wasn't spoken in the same language.

# Chapter 2

## The Misunderstood Wound:
Why Abandonment Exists Even When No One Leaves

When people think of abandonment, they often imagine dramatic scenes a child left in the cold with nothing but a note, a mother leaving her child in the hospital after birth. These images shape how abandonment is commonly understood.

But abandonment is not always loud.
It does not always involve someone leaving.

More often, abandonment happens quietly inside homes that appear stable, within families that function, and in relationships where love exists but emotional closeness does not.

Abandonment does not begin when someone walks away.
It begins when a child's sense of emotional safety becomes uncertain.

Emotional closeness is the experience of feeling seen, understood, and emotionally safe with another person.

It means:

- Someone notices how you feel

- Your emotions are acknowledged rather than dismissed

- You can express yourself without fear of judgment

- You feel secure enough to be vulnerable

- You trust that someone will stay emotionally present

Emotional closeness is not about proximity.
It is about emotional availability.

When emotional closeness is inconsistent or absent, a child doe
not have the ability to understand why.

They only feel the loss.

**How Abandonment Can Begin Without Anyone Leaving**

Children cannot reason through adult circumstances. They do
not understand exhaustion, finances, or emotional overload.
Their world is interpreted through feeling, not logic.

Children are not selfish by nature. They are survival-oriented.
They are wired to seek connection, consistency, and
reassurance.
When those needs are disrupted, they do not analyze the cause.
They simply register the change.

So when emotional availability shifts, the child does not think:

"My parent is overwhelmed."
"They are doing their best."

Their nervous system sense that:

"Something is different."
"They are not as safe as they were before."

That moment, unexplained and unresolved, is where
abandonment begins.

From a psychological perspective, abandonment is not about
what happened.
It is about what the nervous system learned.

The nervous system does not evaluate intent.
It asks only one question:
"Can I trust you to be there?"
When the answer becomes unclear, the body remembers.

**When Both Parents Are Physically Present but Emotionally Unavailable**

The child grows up in a home where both parents are present.

The father works long hours. Some days he leaves before the child wakes and returns after bedtime. When he is home, he is exhausted. He sits quietly, watches television, and keeps to himself. He does not ask about school or emotions, not because he doesn't care, but because he believes providing is enough.

The mother works as well. She manages the household, prepares meals, and keeps everything running. By the time emotions arise, she is depleted.

When the child says she had a bad day, she responds quickly:

- "You'll be fine."

- "It's not that serious."

- "I don't have the energy right now."

No one is cruel.
No one intends harm.
But no one is emotionally available for the child.

From the outside, the home looks stable.

From the inside, something is missing.

**What the Child Experiences**

The child notices the distance.

Not in words.
Not logically.
But emotionally.
No one asks follow-up questions.
No one sits beside them to hear what mattered.

The children do not understand adult stress or responsibility. They only understand:

- Dad is there, but unavailable

- Mom is present, but overwhelmed

- Feelings are inconvenient

- Silence feels safer

What once felt warm now feels distant.
What once felt predictable now feels uncertain.

The father experiences responsibility.
The mother experiences overload.
The child experiences emotional loss.

## The Meaning the Child Makes

Because children cannot reason like adults, they do not think:

"My parents are overwhelmed."

"They're doing their best."

They think:

"I shouldn't need so much."
"My feelings don't matter."
"I'm on my own emotionally."

They stop asking.
They stop sharing.
They stop expecting comfort.

Not because they no longer need it,
but because needing it feels unsafe.

## How This Becomes Abandonment

No one left.

No one intended harm.

But emotional safety became inconsistent.

The child learned:

- Presence does not guarantee connection

- Needs may be inconvenient

- Closeness can disappear

This is how abandonment forms without neglect.
Without cruelty.
Without blame.

## How This Shows Up in Adult Life

As adults, these children may:

- feel unseen in relationships

- struggle to express emotional needs

- react strongly to emotional distance

- minimize their own pain

- feel unsettled without knowing why

They learned early that connection was unreliable.

And because no one explained the emotional shift, the child internalized it.

## Why This Form of Abandonment Is So Hard to See

This type of abandonment is confusing because:

- The parents were loving

- The home was stable

- The child was provided for

- No one intended harm

But trauma is not about intent.
It is about impact.

The child learned to self-soothe too early.
The child learned not to need.
The child learned that closeness could disappear.

That lesson does not fade with time.

## What the Nervous System Learns

Children are wired to detect patterns, not explanations.

When emotional availability becomes inconsistent, the nervous system adapts.

It learns:

- Don't rely too much

- Don't expect too much

- Don't need too much

- Stay alert

- Stay self-contained

This is not weakness.
It is survival.

The child becomes capable, responsible, and independent.

But beneath that strength lives a quiet fear:

**Connection can disappear.** Why You React the Way You Do Now

As an adult:

- Disagreement may feel personal
- Distance may feel threatening
- Emotional conversations may feel unsafe

This is not oversensitivity.

It is a nervous system that learned early that emotional closeness was unpredictable.

Your reactions are not flaws.

They are adaptations.

## Chapter 3:

## Preventing Emotional Abandonment in an Intact Home
*How Emotional Distance Develops and How Parents Can Prevent It*

### 1. Start With the Goal: Connection Over Perfection

**Daily Goal:**
"My child felt seen today."

Parenting is not about getting everything right. It is about making sure your child feels emotionally noticed, valued, and safe even on imperfect days.

### 2. Build a "Hello Ritual" Within the First 10 Minutes

The moment your child sees you matters more than most parents realize. That first interaction sets the emotional tone for the rest of the day or evening.

When your child sees you:

Do:

- Make eye contact and smile, even if you're tired or frustrated. This is how connection is formed.

- Make physical contact
  (hug, hand on the shoulder, fist bump).

- Ask one question to which you will actually listen.

These small moments communicate: "You matter to me."

### 3. Use the 3-Question Check-In (2 Minutes)

Rotate these questions to keep the conversation simple and natural:

1. What was the best part of today?

2. What was the hardest part?

3. Do you want advice, help, or just listening?

This allows your child to feel heard without pressure and teaches emotional awareness over time.

### 4. Validate First. Fix Second.

Most children do not need solutions right away.
They need their feelings recognized.

Avoid saying:

- "You're fine."

- "It's not that serious."

- "Stop crying."

Replace with:

- "That makes sense."

- "I can see why that hurt."

- "I'm here. Tell me more."

### Important Rule:
Validation is not agreement. It is acknowledgment.

You can understand a feeling without approving a behavior.

### 5. Create a Daily "Micro-Moment" of One-on-One Time

Busy parents don't need hours, they need consistency.

Choose 5–10 minutes of uninterrupted time:

- Bedtime talk
- Short walk
- Quick game
- Hair or skin routine • Snack and chat

No phone. No distractions.

**The goal:** Your child feels chosen, not squeezed in.

### 6) Put "emotional availability" on the schedule

Kids interpret unpredictability as danger. So schedule connection like an appointment.

Examples:

- Dad: 7:30–7:45 "Catch-up time"
- Mom: 8:15 "Bedtime check-in"
- Family: Sunday 30-minute "reset"

If it's not planned, it gets replaced.

### 7) Repair quickly when you're tired or you miss the moment

All parents miss moments. The difference is repair.

If you snapped, dismissed, or shut down:

1. **Name it:** "I didn't handle that well."
2. **Own it:** "Sorry about that."

3. **Reconnect:** "Can we try again? Tell me what you were feeling."

## 8) Make emotions safe in your house with simple "rules"

Your children need to know that:

- "Feelings are allowed here."

- "We don't shame emotions."

- "We can be upset and still be respectful."

- "We talk it out after we calm down."

## 9) Let your child see your humanity without making them your therapist

Kids feel less alone when parents model healthy emotion.

**Example:**
"I had a hard day. I'm going to take 10 minutes to breathe, then I'll be ready to talk."

**Avoid:** dumping adult problems onto them.

## 10) Stop "silent parenting" and start narrating love

Some parents love deeply but don't say it. Kids often need to hear the words.

**Say out loud:**

- "I'm proud of you."
- "I love being your parent."
- "I'm glad you're here."
- "I missed you today."

Don't assume they know, teach it.

-

- **Protect Children from Adult Conflict Patterns**

Children do not need to know the details of adult disagreements, but they *do* need reassurance when conflict occurs.

**What to do instead:**

Briefly explain that a disagreement occurred

Reassure the child that it was between adults

Emphasize that the issue has been worked through

Model healthy resolution

**Example script:**

"Your mom and I disagreed earlier, and we were both upset. But we talked it through, and we're okay now. Sometimes adults disagree, but we work it out."

This teaches children: Conflict is normal

Disagreements don't mean relationships are ending

Problems can be resolved respectfully

Emotional safety is restored after tension

When children see conflict handled calmly and followed by repair, they learn that relationships can survive difficult moments. This prevents them from internalizing fear, blame, c responsibility for adult emotions

## 12) Use a weekly "emotional check" like a mini-conferenc

Once a week, ask: "What's one thing we can do better this week?"

## Chapter 4

### When the Mother Leaves and Never Returns
Understanding the Lasting Impact of Maternal Absence

In this chapter, I explore one of the most painful and least talked-about experiences a child can endure: the moment a mother leaves and never truly returns.

This kind of loss does not always happen through death or dramatic abandonment. Sometimes it happens quietly. A mother leaves for work, for opportunity, for survival, or for reasons too complex to explain to a child. She promises to come back. She intends to return. And for a while, the child waits.

But time passes.

And slowly, without anyone ever saying it out loud, the child begins to understand something devastating:

She is not coming back.
It is not about judging mothers or questioning their intentions.
It is about understanding what happens inside a child when the person they are biologically wired to depend on disappears from daily life, emotionally, physically, or both.

When a mother leaves and does not return, the child simply does not miss her.
They lose their sense of safety, consistency, and emotional grounding.
They are left to make sense of a loss they cannot fully understand.

The child learns:

- to stop expecting return

- to stop asking questions

- to stop believing promises

Quietly, a belief forms:

**If I were important, she would have returned.**

They live in emotional suspension, never fully settling, never fully letting go.

And because no one explains the truth, the child creates their own explanations:

- I wasn't important enough

- I was too much

- I was left behind on purpose

Even if the mother loved them.
Even if she meant to return.

The child does not experience

intent. They experience absence.

## What All These Children Learn

The circumstances may differ.
The lesson does not.

Every child learns some version of:

- People leave

- Love is not guaranteed

- I should not need too much

- I should not expect to be chosen

They learn this through silence.
Through repetition.
Through absence.

And because children cannot challenge these beliefs, they grow up carrying them as truth.

## How Maternal Abandonment Shows Up in Adults

Adults who experienced maternal abandonment often struggle with:

- fear of being left

- difficulty trusting others

- hyper-independence

- discomfort receiving care

- intense reactions to rejection

- complicated relationships with women or authority figures

They may crave closeness but fear it.
They may want connection but doubt it will last.

They may say:

- "I don't need anyone."

- "I'm better off alone."

- "People always leave."

Not because they want isolation, but
because attachment once meant pain.

## The Unspoken Grief

Maternal abandonment often goes ungrieved.

No acknowledgment.
No permission to be angry or sad.

The child is told:

- "She did her best."

- "At least you have family."

- "It could have been worse."

So the grief goes underground.

And what cannot be mourned becomes internalized.

## The Truth That Brings Healing

A mother can leave for many reasons.
Some understandable.
Some painful.
Some complex.

But the child's experience still matters.

Healing begins when the adult child can finally say:

"That hurt."
"That loss shaped me." "I
needed more than I received."

Not to blame.
Not to shame.
But to tell the truth.

Because what is finally named loosens its grip. And what is understood no longer controls the story.

## Chapter 5

### When the Father Is Absent
*How Silence Shapes Identity, Security, and Self-Worth*

There are some absences that are easier to explain than others.

A father who leaves.
A father who disappears.
A father who was never meant to stay.

And then there are absences that are never spoken of at all.

When a child is conceived through sperm donation.
When a relationship ends before the child can remember it.
When a father is removed because of trauma, violence, or assault.
When the mother decides, out of protection, pain, or necessity, that the father should not be part of the story.

In these situations, the mother often does what she believes is best.

She says:
"You don't need a father."
"We're enough."
"I'm both parents."
"He wasn't important." "You're
better off without him."

And sometimes, she is right.

But psychology tells us something deeper.

A child does not need a perfect father.
A child does not even need a present father.

What a child needs is permission to wonder.

## The Child Who Learns Not to Ask

In homes where the father is absent by circumstance, donation separation, trauma, the child often senses early that the subject is delicate.

They notice:

- The topic makes their mother tense

- Questions are redirected or shut down

- The story is simplified or avoided

- Curiosity feels uncomfortable

So the child learns quickly:
This is not something I'm supposed to ask about.

They don't want to upset their mother.
They don't want to seem ungrateful.
They don't want to reopen wounds.

So they adapt.

They stop asking.
They stop wondering
They stop expressing curiosity.
And what they learn instead is this:

"My questions are dangerous."

"My curiosity causes pain."

"My needs must be secondary."

This is not emotional maturity.
This is emotional suppression.

## What Psychology Tells Us About This Kind of Loss

From a psychological standpoint, this creates a unique form of abandonment, one that is invisible, complicated, and rarely acknowledged.

The child experiences:

- **Ambiguous loss** (someone who exists but is unreachable)

- **Disenfranchised grief** (grief that is not socially recognized)

- **Attachment disruption without narrative**

There is no story to hold the loss.
No permission to grieve.
No language to explain the absence.

And when grief has no language, the body holds it instead.

## How the Child Interprets the Absence

Even when told, "You don't need a father," the child's nervous system hears something different.

It hears:

- "There is something about this that can't be talked about."

- "This part of me is inconvenient."

- "I should not want what I don't have."

So the child makes an unconscious decision:

I will not need what I am not allowed to want.

This is not strength.
It is survival.

And it shapes identity.

In men especially, this can appear as emotional guardedness, defensiveness, or an inability to tolerate vulnerability.

They may feel anger they can't explain.
Or sadness they can't name.
Or a deep discomfort when others talk about fathers.

Not because they consciously miss someone, but because the body remembers what the mind was told to forget.

**The Silent Contract the Child Makes**

In many of these homes, an unspoken contract forms:

"I won't ask, if you don't have to explain."

The child protects the mother.
The mother protects the child.
And both carry the cost silently.

The mother believes she has spared her child pain.
The child believes they must not need more.

But emotional truth cannot be erased.
It only waits.

**Why This Wound Is So Hard to Recognize**

This type of abandonment is rarely acknowledged because:

- There was no cruelty

- There was no neglect

- The mother often did everything right

- The child was loved

But love does not erase loss.
And protection does not eliminate longing.

A child can feel both grateful and grieving.
Both loved and incomplete.
Both secure and unsettled.

These contradictions confuse the adult mind, but they make perfect sense to the nervous system.

# Chapter 6
## When the Mother Pass Away
### *And No One Speaks Her Name*

There are losses that are acknowledged.
And there are losses that are quietly endured.

The death of a mother is often recognized as tragic.
People bring food.
They offer condolences.
They speak in hushed voices.

But what happens after the
funeral, after the meals stop
coming, after the sympathy fades,
after the world moves on, is where
the real loss begins.

Especially for the child who is left behind.

**The Loss That Could Not Be Spoken**

When a mother dies, the child does not just lose a parent.
They lose their first source of safety.
Their first attachment.
Their emotional anchor.

But in many families, grief is not discussed. Not because it
isn't felt, but because it is too painful for the surviving
parent to hold.

The household becomes quiet.
Careful.
Avoidant.

The surviving parent may say:
"I don't want to talk about it."

"It's too painful."
"We have to be strong."
"Your mother wouldn't want us to be sad."

And so the child learns something devastatingly simple:

My grief is too much for the people I love.

So they stop speaking.

Not because the pain disappears,
but because love requires silence.

**The Child Who Learns to Carry Grief Alone**

When a child is not given permission to grieve openly, they do
something extraordinary and tragic:

They grieve inward.

They become the strong one.
The quiet one.
The child who "handles it well."

They may even comfort the surviving parent.
They may suppress tears.
They may grow up quickly.

And everyone praises their strength.

But inside, something fractures.

Because grief is not meant to be carried alone.
And when it is, it turns into something else.

It turns into:
• emotional numbness
• fear of abandonment

• anxiety around loss

- difficulty expressing needs
- hyper-independence
- emotional guarding

The child learns:
Love can disappear.
People I need can vanish.
I must not get too attached.

## The Unspoken Abandonment

Even when death is unavoidable, the child's nervous system does not understand that.

It only understands:
She was here.
And then she was gone.

And because no one talks about it, because the surviving parent cannot bear the pain, the child is left to make meaning alone.

They may think:

- "If I don't talk about her, I won't hurt anyone."

- "If I don't cry, I'll be okay."

- "If I stay strong, I'll be loved."

This creates a silent form of abandonment:
not by the mother who died, but by the emotional isolation that followed her death.

## How This Loss Shapes the Adult

The child grows up.
Life continues.
But grief does not disappear; it transforms.

As an adult, this child may:

- Fear deep attachment
- Feel unsafe depending on others
- Struggle with vulnerability
- Feel intense anxiety around loss
- Become over self-reliant
- Avoid emotional conversations
- Feel responsible for others' emotions
- Parent from fear rather than trust

They may love deeply but cautiously.
They may give endless but struggle to receive.
They may fear losing their own children in ways they cannot explain.

Because once you lose your mother without support,
the world never feels fully safe again.

**How It Affects Parenting**

Many adults who lost their mother young become deeply devoted parents.

But their parenting often carries quiet fear.

They may:
• Overprotect
• Struggle to tolerate their child's distress
• Feel overwhelmed by their child's dependence
• Fear something terrible will happen
• Feel triggered by their child's sadness

They want to be everything their parent could not be.
But they were never shown how to grieve safely.

So they love from a place of fear rather than security.

## The Grief That Was Never Witnessed

Grief requires witnessing.

It requires someone to say:
"That was hard."
"That mattered."
"You're allowed to miss her."

When that does not happen, grief becomes frozen.

And frozen grief shows up later as:

- anxiety
- emotional numbness
- irritability
- fear of abandonment
- difficulty trusting happiness
- 

Not because the person is broken, but because
their loss was never given language.


## The Healing Begins With Permission

Healing begins when the adult finally allows themselves to say:

I lost my mother, and it changed me.

Not in blame.
Not in anger.
But in truth.

It begins with allowing grief to exist without guilt.
It begins with acknowledging that silence was not strength.
It begins by knowing that survival was not healing.

It begins with understanding that:

You were a child.
You needed comfort.
And you didn't get enough of it.

That matters.

# Chapter 7

## The Misunderstood Wound
### *Loving Someone With an Abandonment Wound*

If you love someone who carries abandonment wounds, you may feel confused, hurt, or emotionally exhausted at times.

You may think:

- "Why do they pull away when I get close?"
- "Why do they react so strongly to small things?"
- "Why does reassurance never seem to be enough?"
- "Why do they shut down instead of talking?"

It's important to understand this:

Their reactions are not about you.
They are about what their nervous system learned long before you arrived.

## What You May Notice in Your Partner

You may see:

- defensiveness during emotional conversations
- withdrawal after conflict
- fear of being misunderstood
- difficulty expressing needs
- strong reactions to perceived rejection
- discomfort with vulnerability

These behaviors are not manipulation.
They are protection.

**What Your Partner Is Often Experiencing Internally**

Even if they don't say it, many people with abandonment wounds carry thoughts like:

- "If I say the wrong thing, I'll lose them."
- "If I need too much, they'll leave."
- "I have to handle this myself."
- "I can't fall apart."

They learned early that closeness could disappear.

So they stay guarded, even when they want connection.

**What Helps:**

- Consistency
- Calm communication
- Emotional predictability
- Reassurance without pressure
- Patience during emotional shutdowns
- Allowing space without withdrawing love

**What Hurts:**

- Threats of leaving
- Dismissing emotions
- Forcing vulnerability
- Interpreting withdrawal as lack of love
- Taking reactions personally

## What Loving Them Requires

Loving someone with abandonment wounds does not mean sacrificing yourself.

It means understanding that:

- Their reactions come from fear, not malice

- Emotional safety matters more than logic

- Trust builds slowly through consistency

- Healing happens in safe relationships.

## The Most Important Truth

Recognizing your limits.

You cannot heal them for them.
You cannot regulate their emotions for them.
You cannot abandon yourself to save them

Healing happens when both people feel safe.

Not perfect.
Not conflict-free.
But emotionally safe.

When the past is no longer being reenacted in the present.
When connection becomes predictable.
When emotional closeness no longer feels dangerous.
That is when abandonment begins to lose its grip.

# Chapter 8

## The Truth That Is Hardest to Accept:
*A Parent's Inability Is Not a Measure of a Child's Worth*

When a child is left, the mind does something very natural and very dangerous: It believes.

*"If the person who created me could leave, something must be wrong with me."*

This belief forms not because it is true but because children do not yet have the ability to understand adult limitation.

Children do not think in terms of capacity, trauma, or readiness. They think in terms of self-blame because that is the only way their world makes sense.

### The Central Truth You Must Understand

Being unwanted by an unprepared parent does not mean you were unworthy of love.

### It means:

- The parent lacked emotional capacity

- The parent was overwhelmed, traumatized, immature, or unstable

- The parent did not have the tools to parent safely

- The parent's life circumstances exceeded their ability to protect or nurture

### Capacity determines behavior, not worth.

- When a Child Is Born Through Trauma or Violence

This is one of the hardest truths to explain, but one of the most important.

When a child is conceived through violence, coercion, or trauma:

- The child may represent unresolved fear or pain
- The parent may experience emotional flooding
- The child becomes a reminder of an event the parent cannot face

This does not mean the child caused the pain.
It means the parent never received the support needed to separate what happened to them from who the child is.

In these cases, the parent is not rejecting the child, they are fleeing their own unhealed trauma.

That distinction matters.

- When Parents Were Unprepared or Emotionally Immature

Some parents leave not because they are cruel but because they are overwhelmed by responsibility they were never prepared to carry.

This includes parents who:
- were very young
- were raised in neglect or abuse
- struggled with addiction
- lacked emotional regulation
- never experienced healthy parenting themselves

These parents often do not leave because they don't care. They leave because they don't know how to stay without breaking.

A child, however, cannot see that.

So the child concludes:

"If they couldn't stay for me, I must not be enough."

That conclusion is understandable, but incorrect.

## The Most Important Message for Healing

Here is the truth that must be gently repeated until it sinks in:

- Your worth was never being evaluated.
- Your parent's capacity was.

A child's value is not measured by:

Whether they were planned

Whether the parent was ready

Whether the parent stayed

Whether the parent healed

A child's worth is inherent.
It is not something that has to be earned, proven, or protected through behavior.

A child does not become worthy because they are well-behaved. They do not earn value by being quiet, compliant, smart, or easy. They are not worthy because someone chooses them.

**They are worthy because they exist.**
A parent leaving says something about:

- their own fear
- their own limitations
- their own trauma
- their own emotional development

It does not define the child.

If worth determined whether parents stayed, then every loving parent would be healthy, stable, and emotionally available.

But that's not reality.

Good people leave.
Loving people fail.
Traumatized people run.
Unhealed people repeat patterns.

And children pay the price, not because they deserved it, but because they were vulnerable.

"You were not left because you were unlovable.
You were left because the person who was supposed to protect you did not have the capacity to do so.
That failure belongs to the circumstance, not to you."

**Why This Is So Hard to Accept**

Because accepting this truth requires letting go of a painful illusion:

That if you were better, they would have stayed.

Letting go of it means facing a harder reality:

You were powerless and it wasn't your fault.

But this truth is also the beginning of healing.

Because once you understand:

- You were not rejected
- You were not defective
- You were worthy

You no longer have to spend your life trying to earn love that should have been given freely.

# Chapter 9

## The Pull Toward The Biological Mother
*When Separation Happens and the Body Remembers*

When a child is separated from a biological parent through adoption, foster care, divorce, incarceration, migration, or fami restructuring, the nervous system registers the loss even when the child is loved, protected, and well cared for by others.

This is not a failure of the caregiver.
It is not evidence that love was insufficient.
It is a biological response to separation from a mother.

The human nervous system is designed to recognize continuity It tracks familiarity through scent, voice, facial structure, movement, rhythm, and mirroring. When those signals are disrupted early in life, the body responds through sensation rather than logic.

This is why a child can be deeply loved by a step-parent, adoptive parent, or extended family member and still experien a sense of longing or disorientation.

The pull is not about affection.
It is about identity and recognition.

Biology does not ask, Who raised you?
It asks, "Where do you come from?

**Why the Pull Persists Even in Loving Homes**

When a biological bond is interrupted before it stabilizes, the nervous system often remains in a state of search.

Even in safe, loving environments, something inside may remain unfinished.

This is why:

- Children may feel drawn to biological parents they never knew

- Adults raised in supportive homes may still feel curiosity or longing

- The pull can feel emotional, urgent, or identity-based

This pull is called unresolved biological processing.

Biological processing describes how the body and nervous system interpret and store experience before conscious thought is involved.

It is not something a person chooses.
It is not something they reason through.
It is something the body does automatically in order to survive.

Long before a child has language or logic, their nervous system is already learning:

- Who responds when I cry?

- What happens when I need comfort?

- Is connection reliable?

- Does closeness feel safe or uncertain?

These experiences are not stored as memories or thoughts. The are stored as patterns of expectation, alertness, tension, and trust.

A child does not analyze situations the way an adult does. The body learns through repetition.

When care is consistent, the nervous system relaxes.
When care becomes unpredictable, the nervous system become alert. When separation or emotional distance happens without explanation, the nervous system prepares for loss.

This process happens automatically, just like pulling a hand aw: from heat. No one teaches it. The body learns because survival depends on it.

So when a child experiences emotional absence, separation, or inconsistency, the nervous system does not ask *why*.

It asks:

- Is this safe?
- Do I need to brace?
- Do I need to protect myself?

The answers to those questions become wired into the body.

**Why the Body Holds On**

The brain stores experiences in two different ways.

Facts are stored as memory.
Emotional experiences are stored in the nervous system.

That is why someone can know they were loved and still feel abandoned. Why someone can understand intellectually that a parent tried their best, yet still react with fear, grief, or longing when connection feels uncertain.

The body is not holding a story. It holds a state of readiness, watchfulness shaped by early experience.

## How It Shows Up Later in Life

Because the nervous system learned through experience, it continues responding as if the original conditions still exist.

This may look like:

- Anxiety when someone pulls away, even briefly
- Strong emotional reactions to distance or change
- Difficulty trusting stability
- Feeling unsafe when relationships shift
- Emotional responses that feel bigger than the moment

These are not overreactions.
They are learned responses.
The body is responding to the present through the lens of the past.

## Why Understanding This Matters

When people don't understand biological processing, they often turn on themselves.

They think:

- I should be over this.
- Nothing that bad happened.
- Why am I still affected?

But the body does not operate on logic or timelines.
It operates on pattern and protection.

Their nervous system learned something early, before language existed, and held onto it to survive.

The body learned how to protect before the mind had words.
Healing does not come from fighting these responses.
It comes from recognizing them for what they are:

Old survival patterns trying to protect a present that no longer requires them.

When this is understood, shame softens.
Self-blame loosens.
And healing becomes possible not through force, but through compassion and consistency.


**The Role of Biology in Attachment**

Pregnancy creates a powerful biological imprint. Hormones such as oxytocin and prolactin shape bonding, while prenatal exposure to the mother's voice and heartbeat establishes familiarity long before birth.

Paternal bonding does not involve gestation, but it does involve genetic recognition and identity formation. Children may seek fathers for mirroring, lineage, or self-understanding.

The pull is not stronger because of gender.
It is expressed differently through biology and socialization.

**What This Means for Healing**

Biology explains why the pull exists and why it persists. Biology does not determine loyalty, love, or emotional commitment.

Without this understanding, the pull toward origin is often misinterpreted as ingratitude, rejection, or betrayal.

In reality, it is none of those things.

The pull toward a biological parent is not proof of love. It is proof of a nervous system doing exactly what it was designed to do.

Understanding this distinction allows caregivers to release misplaced guilt and allows individuals to explore their origins without destroying the relationships that sustained them.

Nothing was missing in their love.
Nothing is wrong with the child.
This was biology, not ungratefulness.

**The Biological Pull Toward Origin**

Across cultures and family structures, people often describe a powerful pull toward biological parents, an internal force that feels emotional, instinctive, and sometimes confusing.

Biology does not frame this pull as destiny or proof of love. It explains it as recognition.

At its core, this pull is not about affection. It is about identity and survival wiring.

From an evolutionary standpoint, humans are wired for genetic continuity. The nervous system recognizes biological sameness through scent, voice, facial structure, movement, and later through identity formation. Even without conscious awareness the body responds to these cues.

This is why:
• Children may feel drawn to biological parents they never kne
• Adults raised in loving homes may still feel curiosity or longir

• The pull can feel urgent, emotional, or identity-based rather than relational

Biology does not ask Who raised you?
It asks Where do you come from?

What This Means for Healing

Biology explains:
• Why the pull exists
• Why it persists
• Why it does not disappear with time or logic

Biology does *not* determine loyalty, love, or emotional connection.

Those are shaped by lived experience.

Without this framework, the pull toward origin is often misinterpreted as ingratitude, betrayal, or rejection. In reality, i is a neutral biological response, not a moral failure.

The pull toward a biological parent is not proof of love.

It is proof of the nervous system doing what it was designed t do.

Understanding this distinction allows people to explore their origins without destroying the relationships that raised them, and without turning survival responses into sources of shame.

## Chapter 10

## Good Intentions, Lasting Absence
### Why Care Does Not Always Heal Separation

Many people grow up with a familiar explanation to elevate their pain:

*You were loved.*
*They did their best.*
*You were safe.*

These statements may be true.
But they are different from healing.

This chapter is not about whether love existed.
It is about why love, effort, and sacrifice do not always resolve the impact of separation.

Because care and healing are not the same thing.

When Love Exists but Loss Remains

Care protects survival.
Healing restores emotional continuity.

A child can be clothed, fed, educated, and protected and still carry the imprint of loss. Separation changes the emotional landscape of a child's life. Even when a new caregiver provides stability, the original rupture does not automatically resolve.

This is why children raised in loving homes may still carry grief they cannot name.

**Why Good Intentions Do Not Always Reach the Wound**
Adults often assume that explanation should bring closure.

"If they understood why, they would be okay."

But attachment does not operate through explanation.
It operates through felt safety over time.

A child can intellectually understand:

- that a parent was overwhelmed

- that circumstances were difficult

- that the separation was necessary

And still feel the loss.

The child learns:

- My sadness makes others uncomfortable

- My questions are unwelcome

- My loss should not be mentioned

Over time, grief does not disappear.
It simply goes underground.

Later in life, it often resurfaces as:

**Unexplained Sadness**

She wakes up with a heavy feeling in her chest, even though
nothing is technically wrong. She has a husband that adores her
and children. The bills are paid. Her life looks fine from the
outside. Yet the sadness lingers uninvited, unexplained. She
can't point to a single moment or memory that caused it. It just
is. Later, someone asks, "What's wrong?" and she says,
"Nothing," because she truly doesn't know how to explain a
feeling that has no clear beginning. The sadness doesn't scream
it hums softly in the background of her life.

## 2. Fear of Loss

Every time she gets close to someone, she braces herself. Not because she expects betrayal, but because she expects disappearance. When people don't text back right away, her mind fills in the silence with endings.

She loves deeply, but quietly. Carefully. Always holding back just enough so that if they leave, it won't completely destroy her. She tells herself she's being realistic, but deep down, she knows she's protecting an old wound that never healed.

## 3. Difficulty Trusting Closeness

When someone shows genuine care, she becomes uncomfortable. Compliments feel suspicious. Kindness feels temporary.

She finds herself pulling away when things feel too warm, too safe. Not because she doesn't want connection, but because closeness once came with disappointment, inconsistency, or emotional withdrawal.

So she keeps people at arm's length, not realizing she's guarding a younger version of herself who learned that attachment often led to pain.

## 4. Guilt for Wanting More

She tells herself she should be grateful. Others had it worse. She had food, clothes, and a roof over her head.

Yet something inside her still feels empty. When she wants more affection, more emotional safety, more acknowledgment, she feels ashamed.

She wonders if she's being selfish or ungrateful. She silences her own needs before anyone else can. What she doesn't realize is that wanting more doesn't mean she wasn't given enough, it means she's human.

## 5. Confusion About One's Own Emotions

When people ask how she feels, she freezes. Not because she doesn't have feelings, but because she can't name them.
Is it sadness? Anger? Disappointment?
She was never taught how to sort through emotions, only how to endure them. So she second-guesses herself constantly, unsure whether her reactions are valid or exaggerated. Over time, she learns to trust logic more than feeling because feelings once felt unsafe or inconvenient to express.

Not because the person is ungrateful, but because the loss was never allowed language.

### When Children Protect the Adults Who Raised Them

Many adults hesitate to name their pain because they fear it will sound like blame.

They worry:

- It will invalidate the love they received

- It will hurt the people who cared for them

- It will make them seem unappreciative

So they stay silent.

They protect the caregivers emotionally, even long after childhood has ended.

This silence often delays healing. Not because the caregiver did something wrong but because the child never had permission or gave themselves permission to name what was missing.

In cases of separation, children often carry a quiet question:

*Did my mother think about me?*

The truth is more complex than most people realize.

Some mothers experience deep emotional pain but lack the capacity, support, or stability to remain present.
Some cope by emotionally shutting down.
Some distance themselves because the pain of connection is too overwhelming.

From the outside, this can look like indifference.

To the child, it often feels like rejection.

But separation does not always mean lack of love.
Sometimes it reflects emotional limitation, psychological overwhelm, or circumstances beyond the mother's ability to manage.

The child, however, rarely sees this complexity.

They draw the conclusion that feels most logical:
*If I were more lovable, this wouldn't have happened.*

A child can be loved and still feel abandoned.
A parent can care deeply and still be unable to stay.
Both experiences can be true at the same time.

Healing begins when we stop forcing one truth to erase the other.

# Chapter 11

## Gratitude and Grief Can Coexist
*The Emotional Contradiction Few Are Allowed to Name*

Gratitude is often taught as the cure for pain.

If someone stepped in, cared for you, and gave you a life that looked stable, gratitude becomes the expected response. It is praised. It is rewarded. It is used as proof that everything turned out fine.

Grief, however, is rarely invited into that story.

For many people who were separated from a parent, gratitude not a feeling, it is a requirement. It becomes something you perform to reassure others that their sacrifices mattered, that their love was enough, that nothing important was lost. Over time, gratitude can begin to crowd out other emotions, not because those emotions disappear, but because there is no safe place for them to exist.

This is where the contradiction begins.

You can feel thankful for the people who raised you and still mourn what never was. You can appreciate the care you received and still ache for the bond that was interrupted. These emotions do not cancel each other out, yet many people are taught that they should.

Grief in these circumstances often goes unnamed. It does not come with a clear event or a socially recognized loss. There may be no public permission to mourn, no shared language to explain what hurts. Instead, the grief lives quietly beneath the surface, surfacing in moments of transition, intimacy, or reflection.

What makes this grief especially complicated is loyalty.

Many people fear that naming their grief will sound like ingratitude. They worry it will hurt the people who stayed, invalidate the care they received, or suggest that something better was deserved. As a result, they learn to edit themselves. They express appreciation freely, while carefully managing or suppressing sadness.

Over time, this emotional imbalance takes a toll.

Gratitude that is not freely chosen can become heavy. It can turn into pressure, obligation, or silence. Grief that is not acknowledged does not disappear; it finds other ways to speak. It may show up as restlessness, resentment, emotional distance, or confusion about one's own feelings.

This chapter exists to name what many people experience but rarely say aloud: gratitude and grief are not opposites. They are parallel truths. One reflects what was given. The other reflects what was lost.

Allowing both to exist is not a betrayal. It is an act of emotional honesty.

Gratitude honors the people who showed up.
Grief honors the part of the story that did not get a chance to unfold.

Healing does not require choosing one over the other. It begins when both are given permission to speak.

# Chapter 12

## Clinging to the Hope of Origin
*When Idealized Parents Feel Safer Than Real Ones*

For some people who have experienced abandonment, hope becomes a place to live.

Not hope in the future but hope in the past the belief that somewhere, someone exists who would have stayed if circumstances had been different. This hope is rarely spoken aloud, yet it shapes emotions, decisions, and relationships in powerful ways.

The idea of an idealized parent often feels safer than engaging fully with the people who are present.

This is not because the real people are unloving.
It is because hope carries less risk than reality.

## Why Idealized Parents Feel Safe

An idealized parent cannot disappoint you.

They cannot reject you again.
They cannot fail you in new ways.
They cannot misunderstand you or leave when things get hard.

Because they are imagined, they remain perfect.

For someone who has experienced abandonment, this imagined parent becomes a safe emotional container. The nervous system can attach without the threat of loss. There is no need to negotiate boundaries, manage conflict, or tolerate disappointment.

Hope becomes a form of emotional control.

## The Difference Between Curiosity and Idealization

Wanting to understand one's origins is natural. Curiosity seeks information. Idealization seeks safety.

Curiosity asks:
*Who are they? What is my story?*

Idealization asks something deeper:
*Who would I have been if I had never been left?*

When idealization takes hold, the absent parent is no longer just a person. They become a symbol of wholeness, belonging, and an unbroken beginning.

This symbol can feel more comforting than any real relationship.

## Why Real Relationships Feel Riskier

Real relationships require vulnerability. They involve disagreement, unmet expectations, and emotional exposure. For someone with abandonment history, these moments can reactivate fear.

Real people can leave.
Real people can disappoint.
Real people can hurt you without meaning to.

An idealized parent exists outside these risks. They remain untouched by daily life, conflict, and reality. The nervous system relaxes around them because there is nothing to lose.

## When Hope Becomes a Substitute for Attachment

Over time, clinging to the hope of origin can quietly replace present attachment.

A person may:

- Emotionally withdraw from caregivers or family
- Minimize the importance of relationships that require effort
- Fantasize about reunification without preparation for reality
- Feel disappointed or disconnected even in loving relationships

The hope becomes a refuge, not a bridge.

This does not mean the person wants to abandon those who stayed. It means they are protecting themselves from emotional risk.

### How Idealization Can Distort the Past

Idealized parents are often imagined as wiser, kinder, or more capable than they were. Their absence is reframed as tragic or misunderstood. The family who stayed may be remembered as imperfect, restrictive, or emotionally unsafe by comparison.

This shift is rarely intentional.

It is the mind's way of making the loss feel meaningful rather than random.

### The Collision Between Fantasy and Reality

When contact with a biological parent eventually occurs, the emotional impact can be jarring.

The parent may not match the image that sustained the hope. They may be limited, unavailable, or deeply human. For some, this is devastating. For others, it is clarifying.

What often hurts most is not the person, it is the loss of the fantasy.

## Why Letting Go of Idealization Is So Hard

Letting go of an idealized parent can feel like losing the relationship all over again, even if it never truly existed.

The fantasy served a purpose. It held pain. It protected hope. It gave the nervous system a place to rest.

Releasing it can feel unsafe, lonely, and destabilizing.

# Chapter 13

## Rewriting the Past to Make the Pain Make Sense
*Why Some Survivors Turn Against the Ones Who Stayed*

When pain has no clear explanation, the mind looks for one.

For many survivors of abandonment, the original loss does not come with a story that feels complete or survivable. There is separation, but no satisfying reason. There is grief, but no clear place to put it. Over time, this unresolved pain creates pressure an internal demand for meaning.

When meaning cannot be found, it is sometimes created.

This is where the past begins to change.

### The Need for a Coherent Story
Human beings need their lives to make sense. Especially when something painful happens early, the mind tries to organize memory into a narrative that explains why things unfolded the way they did.?

When the original abandonment feels too complex, random, or painful to hold, the mind may begin to revise the story subtly at first, then more firmly. It is an attempt to survive confusion.

### Why the Ones Who Stayed Become Targets

Turning toward the people who stayed can feel safer than turning toward the ones who left.

The absent parent is often emotionally distant, unreachable, or idealized. There is little opportunity to express anger there. The caregivers who stayed, however, are present. They are human.

They can be confronted.

And so, the pain moves.

The family who provided care may slowly be reinterpreted as controlling, emotionally limiting, or responsible for what was lost. Past moments are reexamined. Memories are reshaped. Neutral experiences are filtered through adult pain.

This shift is rarely conscious.

It is easier to direct anger toward those who remained than to face the grief of those who were gone.

### How Rewriting the Past Creates Emotional Relief

Blame can feel stabilizing.

When pain is given a clear source, it becomes easier to carry. Confusion is replaced with certainty. Grief is replaced with anger. Vulnerability is replaced with control.

Rewriting the past can provide temporary relief by:

- Offering a reason for the loss
- Assigning responsibility
- Reducing the feeling of helplessness
- Protecting the idealized image of the absent

parent In this version of the story, the survivor is no longer powerless. They are reacting to injustice.


### When Gratitude Turns Into Resentment

For many survivors, gratitude was expected early. They were told to be thankful, compliant, appreciative. Over time, unexpressed grief accumulates beneath that gratitude.

The caregivers who stayed may be blamed for enforcing silence, even if they never intended to do so.

This resentment is not about the present.
It is about what was never named in the past.

## The Cost of This Rewrite

Although rewriting the past can feel empowering at first, it comes with consequences.

Relationships fracture.
Communication shuts down.
Understanding is replaced with certainty.

The survivor may feel temporarily stronger, but also increasingly isolated. The story that once provided relief begins to limit connection. Complexity is lost. Compassion narrows.

The pain has a place, but it no longer has a path forward.

## What Is Often Lost in the Rewrite

When survivors turn against those who stayed, they may lose access to important truths:

- That care and harm can coexist
- That protection does not erase loss
- That silence can wound without intention
- That grief does not require a villain

Most importantly, they lose the ability to hold more than one truth at a time.

## Healing Requires Expanding the Story, Not Replacing It

Healing does not mean defending caregivers at the expense of the survivor's pain. It means allowing the story to become more honest and more complex.

This includes recognizing:

- The loss was real
- The pain mattered
- The caregivers were imperfect and human
- The absence cannot be fully explained by blame

When the past no longer needs to be rewritten to make the pain tolerable, the survivor gains something more valuable than certainty.

They gain freedom.

## A Closing Truth

Turning against the ones who stayed is rarely about hatred. It is about unresolved grief searching for meaning.

The pain does not need a new story to be valid. It needs space, language, and compassion.

Healing begins when the past is allowed to be complex, and when the survivor no longer has to choose between truth and connection.

## Chapter: 14
## The Silence of Forbidden Love
*When Shame Makes Absence Feel Safer Than Staying*

There are some losses that come with explanations.
And there are others that come with nothing at all.

For children who are intentionally left behind, especially when the separation is tied to betrayal, secrecy, or shame, the absence carries a different weight. There is no clear story to hold onto. No goodbye that makes sense. No narrative that allows the mind to rest.

Only questions.

Why didn't they stay?
Why didn't they try?
Why was it easier to disappear than to be my parent?

This kind of abandonment leaves a particular wound because it does not just remove a person, it removes understanding. The child grows up trying to make sense of something they were never given the tools to understand.

And when the parent who left never explains, never repairs, and never returns emotionally, the child is left to do the meaning of making sense alone.

### When a Parent Leaves Out of Shame

Not all abandonment is rooted in lack of love.
Some of it is rooted in shame.

Shame is one of the most powerful forces in human behavior. It does not encourage repair, it encourages hiding. It convinces people that if they stay, they will be exposed, judged, or forced to face the harm they caused.

For some parents, especially fathers who never bonded early or who associate fatherhood with failure or loss of control, shame becomes unbearable. Instead of moving toward the child, they move away from anything that reminds them of their mistakes.

The child becomes a mirror into which they cannot look.

This does not mean the child was unwanted.
It means the parent lacked the emotional capacity to face themselves.

But to a child, none of this is visible.

All they experience is absence.

### The Psychological Impact of Being Left Without Explanation

When a parent leaves without emotional closure, the child's nervous system is left in a state of unresolved grief. The brain cannot process what it does not understand, so it fills in the blanks.

Often, the conclusion becomes:
*It must be me.*

Children are wired to believe that caregivers are necessary for survival. When a caregiver disappears, the child does not assume the parent is incapable. They assume they are the problem.

This belief settles quietly and can follow them into adulthood.

It may show up as:

- Difficulty trusting that people will stay

- A deep fear of abandonment

- Hyper-independence

- Over-functioning in relationships

- A constant search for approval

- A lingering sense of being "unchosen"

And because the loss was never explained, the grief never had a place to land.

## Why the Questions Never Stop

Many adults who were abandoned this way find themselves asking the same questions over and over:

What made you leave?
What did you tell yourself to make it okay?
Why didn't you fight for me?
Did I matter at all?

These are not questions of blame.
They are questions of identity.

The child is not asking for justification.
They are trying to understand their place in the world.

And when no answers come, the nervous system holds the question open indefinitely.

## What Psychology Understands About This Kind of Loss

When abandonment happens without emotional acknowledgment, the brain stores the experience as unfinished.

There is:

- No emotional resolution

- No narrative completion

- No sense of safety restored

This is why the pain can resurface years later often during major life events like becoming a parent, entering a committed relationship, or experiencing loss.

The body remembers what the mind was never allowed to process.

And often, the grief intensifies not because the loss is new, but because the person is finally old enough, safe enough, or strong enough to feel it.

## What the Child Needs to Hear

There are things many children who were separated from their mother never hear, but desperately need to hear:

You were not left because you were unlovable.
You were not left because you were difficult.
You were not left because you weren't enough.

You were left because the person who left did not know how to stay.

Some parents carry so much shame that they choose disappearance over responsibility.
Some avoid because facing the child would mean facing themselves.
Some never developed the emotional capacity to bond in a healthy way.

None of that belongs to the child.

## When Closure Does Not Come From the Parent

One of the hardest truths to accept is that closure does not always come from the person who caused the wound.

Some parents will never explain.
Some will never apologize.

Some will never acknowledge the impact of their absence.

And waiting for that moment can keep a person emotionally stuck for years.

Healing begins when the child, now an adult understands this:

Closure is not something they give you.
It is something you allow yourself.

It comes from understanding the why without excusing the harm.
From grieving what was lost without minimizing it.
From separating your worth from someone else's limitations.

## What Healing Looks Like Here

Healing does not mean forgetting.
It does not mean pretending the pain didn't exist.
And it does not mean reconciling at all costs.

Healing means:

- Accepting that the absence was real

- Naming the grief without shame

- Releasing the belief that you caused it

- Allowing yourself to mourn what you never received

- Choosing to build safety within yourself and your relationships

It means understanding that your longing was valid.
Your pain was justified.
And your need for connection was human.

## How the Adult Child Begins to Heal

Healing from this kind of abandonment does not happen all at once. It happens in small, intentional shifts daily choices that slowly teach the nervous system something new: I am safe now. I am allowed to exist fully. I do not have to earn love.

Below are ways an adult child can begin that process, gently and realistically.

### 1. Name What Happened Without Minimizing It

Healing begins with honesty.

This means allowing yourself to say:

- *I was hurt.*

- *Something important was missing.*

- *That loss mattered to me.*

Not with blame.
Not with anger.
But with clarity.

Many adult children try to heal while minimizing their experience. They say things like:
"It wasn't that bad."
"Others had it worse."
"I should be over it."

But healing does not come from comparison.
It comes from acknowledgment.

You do not need to prove your pain to anyone for it to be real.

### 2. Separate Your Worth From the Parent's Absence

This is one of the most important daily practices.

Each time the thought appears: *If I had been enough, they would have stayed...*

Gently replace it with:
*Their leaving was about their limits, not my worth.*

This may feel unnatural at first.
That's because your nervous system learned a different story early on.

Repetition matters.
The brain rewires through consistency, not insight alone.

### 3. Create Emotional Safety in Small, Predictable Ways

Your body learned unpredictability.
Healing comes from consistency.

This might look like:

- Keeping simple routines

- Going to bed at the same time

- Eating regularly

- Spending time with people who feel calm and steady

- Saying no to emotional chaos

Safety is not dramatic.
It is quiet.
It is boring.
And it is deeply regulating.

### 4. Allow Yourself to Grieve What You Didn't Get

Grief is not only about death.
It is about absence.

You may need to grieve:

- The parent who wasn't able to stay

- The protection you didn't receive

- The explanations you never got

- The version of childhood you imagined

Grief may come as sadness.
Or anger.
Or numbness.
Or sudden tears.

None of them is wrong.

Letting yourself feel it, without rushing it away is part of healing.


## 5. Stop Seeking Closure From the Person Who Cannot Give It

This step is painful, but freeing.

If someone has never taken responsibility, never explained, or never shown emotional availability, waiting for them to change keeps the wound open.

Healing does not require:

- An apology

- A confession

- An explanation

It requires acceptance of what is, not what should have been.

You are allowed to stop waiting.

## 6. Reparent Yourself in the Ways You Needed Most

This is not about pretending to be your own parent.
It is about meeting needs that went unmet.

You can begin to:

- Speak to yourself with reassurance instead of criticism

- Validate your emotions instead of dismissing them

- Offer yourself comfort instead of pushing through pain

- Set boundaries without guilt

- Celebrate your achievements, even small ones

These acts teach the nervous system something new:
*I am cared for now.*

## 7. Choose Relationships That Feel Safe, Not Familiar

Sometimes the hardest realization is this:
What feels familiar is not always what feels healthy.

Many adult children of abandonment unconsciously gravitate
toward emotionally unavailable people because that pattern feels
known.

Healing means learning to choose:

- Consistency over intensity

- Safety over excitement

- Presence over potential

This takes time.
And patience.
And compassion for yourself.

## 8. Let Healing Be Slow

There is no timeline for healing abandonment.
There is no finish line.

Some days will feel strong.
Others will feel tender.

Progress often looks like:

- Reacting less

- Recovering faster

- Understanding yourself more deeply

- Feeling less shame about your needs

That is growth.

## A Final Grounding Truth

You did not imagine the pain.
You did not cause the loss.
And you are not broken because it still affects you.

Healing is not about forgetting.
It is about finally giving yourself what you were once denied:
understanding, safety, and care.

And every small step you take toward yourself, every
boundary, every moment of self-compassion, is proof
that the story does not end with abandonment.

# Chapter 15

## When Love Needed Translation: A Son's Letter to His Father

Dad,

I'm writing this with respect, honesty, and care.

I want to start by saying something that matters I know you tried. I know you showed love in the ways you understood by working hard, by providing, by protecting, by doing what you believed a good father was supposed to do. I never doubted tha you cared about me or wanted the best for my life.

What I'm trying to share isn't about blame. It's about helping you understand what it felt like to grow up as your son.

You didn't have a father to show you how to do this. I know that shaped you. You built your version of fatherhood from survival, responsibility, and duty. From your point of view, being present meant showing up, paying bills, keeping things together, and making sure nothing fell apart. I see that now.

As a child, though, I didn't understand pressure, exhaustion, or the weight you carried. I didn't know what it meant to be overwhelmed or unsure of how to show emotion. I only knew what it felt like to be on the other side of it.

Sometimes, when you were quiet, busy, or focused on fixing things, I felt unsure of where I fit emotionally. I didn't always know when it was okay to talk, to need reassurance, or to make mistakes. I learned early to be careful, to handle things on my own, and to not take up too much space.

I know you weren't trying to be distant. But from a child's point of view, distance doesn't look like intention, it feels like uncertainty. I needed comfort, encouragement, and words that told me I was doing okay, even when I struggled. I needed to know that making mistakes wouldn't change how you saw me.

When I succeeded, I often felt like it was expected. When I struggled, I felt noticed. That taught me to push myself hard and hide the parts of me that felt unsure. I carried that into adulthood, often measuring my worth by what I could do instead of who I was.

I understand now that your way of loving came from what you never received. You did the best you could with the tools you had. And at the same time, there were things I needed that neither of us knew how to name back then.

I'm not writing this to reopen the past. I'm writing because I believe understanding can still matter. I believe relationships can grow even later in life. And I believe that knowing how it felt for me doesn't erase what you did, it adds context to it.

What I needed most was to feel emotionally safe with you. To know that I could talk without disappointing you. To feel encouraged, not just corrected. To know that I was already enough.

I hope this letter helps you see me more clearly not as a failure, not as ungrateful, but as a child who was learning in the same house in which you were surviving.

I love you. And I believe it's still possible to understand each other better now.

Your son

# Chapter 16

## The Same Wound, Different Armor
*The Adult Who Learned to Live Without Asking*

By the time the child becomes an adult, the loss no longer feels like a memory.

It feels like a personality.

The adult may not think of themselves as someone who experienced abandonment. In fact, many adults who grew up without emotional attunement describe their childhood as "fine." They function well. They are responsible. They handle life.

But something beneath the surface feels strained.

They carry a quiet tension they cannot name.
A restlessness.
A sense of emotional distance from others even from those the love.

This chapter is about that adult.

### The Adult Who Learned to Be Self-Sufficient Too Early

The adult child of emotional absence often becomes highly capable.

They manage their lives well.
They solve problems quickly.
They rarely ask for help.

On the surface, they appear strong.

But this strength was learned under pressure.

They learned early that their needs would not always be met.

That emotions complicated things.
That depending on others could lead to disappointment.

So they adapted.

They became:

- self-reliant

- emotionally contained

- independent to a fault

- uncomfortable needing anyone

They do not see this as a wound.
They see it as maturity.

But self-sufficiency that develops too early is not confidence, it is protection.

## How Unspoken Loss Shapes Adult Behavior

When emotional loss was never acknowledged, the adult develops coping strategies that feel normal to them but confusing to others.

### They minimize their own pain

They say things like:

- "It wasn't that bad."

- "Other people had it worse."

- "I'm fine."

They learned long ago that their pain had nowhere to go.

### They struggle to ask for help

Even when overwhelmed, they hesitate.

Asking feels like burdening someone.
They prefer to manage alone even when exhausted.

**They stay emotionally guarded**

They may care deeply but reveal little.
They share facts, not feelings.
They keep conversations safe and surface-level.

Vulnerability feels risky because it once led to disappointment.


## How This Shows Up in Relationships

In relationships, the adult child of emotional absence often experiences confusion.

They may want closeness but feel uncomfortable when it actually appears.
They may crave connection but pull away when someone gets too close.
They may struggle to express needs, then feel hurt when those needs go unmet.

They often think:

- "I shouldn't need this."

- "I don't want to be difficult."

- "I'll just handle it myself."

When conflict arises, they may shut down or become defensive not because they don't care, but because emotional intensity feels unsafe.

They were never taught how to sit inside emotional discomfor with another person.

**The Hidden Fear Beneath the Coping**

Beneath the independence, the restraint, and the emotional control is often a quiet fear:

If I need too much, I'll be left.

So the adult learns to need less.

They soften their wants.
They lower expectations.
They convince themselves they are "low maintenance."

But what they are really doing is protecting themselves from loss, they never learned how to grieve.

**Why the Adult Often Feels "Different"**

Many adults who grew up this way describe a vague sense of being uncoordinated with others.

They may:

- feel disconnected even in close relationships

- struggle to feel deeply relaxed around others

- feel uneasy receiving care

- feel uncomfortable when someone focuses on their emotions

They often function well in practical life but feel unsure how to navigate emotional closeness.

This is not because they lack emotion.
It is because emotion once felt unsafe to express.

**The Cost of Carrying It Alone**

Over time, this emotional self-reliance can lead to:

- burnout

- loneliness

- difficulty trusting others

- resentment in relationships

- emotional numbness

- chronic tension

Not because the person is broken, but because humans are not meant to carry emotional weight alone.

The cost of silence is cumulative.

**What Begins to Change in Adulthood**

Healing begins when the adult starts to notice patterns instead of judging themselves.

When they begin to see:

- how often they minimize their needs

- how quickly they withdraw

- how uncomfortable vulnerability feels

- how much effort they put into appearing "fine"

This awareness alone can be powerful.

Because once something is seen, it can be examined.
And once it is examined, it can be softened.

**The Shift From Survival to Choice**

The adult child does not need to relive the past.

They need to understand how it shaped them.

They need to recognize that:

- their coping made sense

- their adaptations were intelligent

- their nervous system learned to survive

And that what once kept them safe may now be limiting connection.

The goal is not to become dependent.
It is to become **secure enough to choose connection** rather than avoid it.

**The Quiet Truth**

Many adults spend years trying to "fix" themselves without realizing there is nothing broken.

They are not weak.
They are not distant.
They are capable of love.

They are simply people who learned early how to live without emotional support.

And now, they are learning slowly, carefully, that they no longer have to.


**How Men and Women Often Carry Abandonment Differently**

While the wound of abandonment may begin the same way, the way it is expressed in adulthood often differs, largely because men and women are taught very different rules about emotion, strength, and vulnerability.

These differences are not biological flaws.
They are learned responses shaped by culture, expectation, and survival.

## How Men Are Often Conditioned to Cope

From a young age, many boys are taught directly or indirectly that emotional expression is weakness.

They are praised for:

- being strong

- being independent

- staying composed

- not needing help

They are discouraged from:

- crying

- expressing fear

- admitting emotional need

- appearing vulnerable

So when a boy experiences emotional absence or loss, he often learns to handle it by **shutting down,** not reaching out.

As an adult, this often shows up as:

## Emotional Containment

He keeps emotions controlled and private.
He may struggle to articulate what he feels.
He often believes emotions should be managed alone.

**Sensitivity to Respect**

Because emotional expression was discouraged, respect becomes the acceptable emotional currency.

When he feels ignored, dismissed, or criticized, it doesn't register as hurt, it registers as disrespect.

His reaction may look like:

- defensiveness

- irritation

- withdrawal

- emotional shutdown

Not because he wants control, but because being emotionally exposed feels unsafe.

**Difficulty With Emotional Conversations**

He may become uncomfortable when feelings are discussed openly.
Not because he doesn't care, but because he was never taught *how* to engage emotionally.

Emotional conversations may feel:

- overwhelming

- confusing

- threatening to his sense of competence

So he changes the subject, becomes quiet, or shuts down.

**The Cultural Message He Learned**

*Be strong.*
*Don't complain.*

*Handle it yourself.*
*Needing others is weakness.*

As a result, many men experience abandonment not as sadness but as frustration, anger, or emotional distance.

## How Women Are Often Conditioned to Cope

Girls, on the other hand, are often taught that connection is central to their value.

They are encouraged to:

- be emotionally aware

- be nurturing

- maintain harmony

- prioritize relationships

So when emotional abandonment occurs, they often respond b Over-accommodating rather than withdrawing.

As adults, this often shows up as:

### Hyper-Awareness of Others

They notice shifts in mood, tone, and energy.
They scan for signs of disconnection.
They take responsibility for emotional balance.

### Fear of Being Too Much

They hesitate to express needs.
They minimize their feelings.
They worry about overwhelming others.

They often think:

- "I don't want to be a burden."
- "I should be grateful."
- "I'll just deal with it myself."

## Emotional Over-Functioning

They may:

- over-explain
- over-apologize
- over-give
- over-accommodate

They try to maintain closeness by being emotionally useful.

## The Cultural Message She Learned

Be understanding.
Be accommodating.
Keep the peace.
Don't ask for too much.

As a result, many women experience abandonment as anxiety, self-doubt, or emotional overextension.

## The Same Wound, Two Different Expressions

Though men and women often look different in how they cope, the underlying fear is the same:

If I need too much, I will lose connection.

Men often protect themselves by withdrawing.
Women often protect themselves by over-giving.

Both are attempts to prevent loss.

Both are survival strategies.

**Why These Patterns Persist in Adulthood**

These behaviors are reinforced by society.

Men are praised for emotional restraint.
Women are praised for emotional labor.

So the patterns go unnoticed and often unchallenged.

But underneath both responses is the same unresolved question

Am I safe to be fully seen and still be loved?

Until that question is answered through experience, the nervou
system continues to operate from protection rather than trust.

**What Changes When This Is Understood**

When adults recognize these patterns, something shifts.

Men begin to see that vulnerability is not weakness it is
regulation.
Women begin to see that self-abandonment is not love it is fear

Understanding replaces self-criticism.
Compassion replaces shame.
Choice replaces instinct.

And that is where healing begins.

# Chapter 17

## When Love Is Earned. Not Expected
### *How Abandonment Shapes Adult Relationships*

Many adults who have experienced abandonment do not enter relationships believing love will simply be there.

They enter believing it must be maintained, protected, and constantly reinforced. Love feels conditional, fragile, and easy to lose. As a result, they often give more than is asked, more than is fair, and more than is healthy because boundaries once felt dangerous.

It's the nervous system way of saying: connection is not guaranteed.

## Why They Give More Than They Should

Adults with abandonment histories often become the ones who do the most in relationships. They stay late. They try harder. They forgive quickly. They adjust themselves endlessly to keep others comfortable.

This behavior is not accidental. It is a learned survival response.

They often:

- Overextend emotionally and practically
- Take responsibility for other people's moods
- Apologize even when they are not wrong
- Minimize their own needs to preserve harmony

They belief that the relationship's survival depends primarily on them.

Many abandonment survivors slide into the role of emotional caretaker. They sense shifts in tone. They anticipate conflict. They try to prevent discomfort before it happens.

This develops because, early on, emotional safety depends on adaptation. Being attentive kept connection intact. Being easy made relationships last.

As adults, this can look like:

- Managing the emotional climate of the relationship
- Putting their partner's needs first as a default
- Avoiding difficult conversations to prevent distance
- Believing that love requires endurance They confuse effort with security.

Abandonment survivors often recognize harmful behavior but stay anyway.

They may overlook:

- Emotional unavailability
- Inconsistent affection
- Broken promises
- Disrespect framed as "flaws"

This is not denial. It is fear. For someone with abandonment history, leaving can feel as threatening as being left. Ending a relationship may activate the same survival alarm as early loss. Staying, even in pain, can feel safer than risking separation.

**When Boundaries Feel Like Risk**

From the outside, these individuals may look like "doormats." From the inside, they are carefully managing perceived danger.

Boundaries feel risky because:

- Conflict can lead to distance
- Distance can lead to loss
- Loss feels unbearable

They bend, absorb, and tolerate as a survival response, an effort to reduce perceived threat, not a reflection of low self-respect.

## The Emotional Cost of Over-Giving

Over time, this way of loving becomes exhausting.

The survivor may feel:

- Emotionally depleted
- Quietly resentful
- Invisible within the relationship
- Disconnected from their own needs

The relationship may continue, but the person slowly disappears inside it. And despite all the giving, there is no guarantee the other person will stay.

## What Healing Begins to Shift

Healing does not require becoming less loving. It requires becoming less afraid.

As abandonment wounds are addressed, survivors begin to learn:

- Love does not need to be earned
- Boundaries do not cause abandonment
- Leaving harm is different from being left
- Reciprocity is safer than sacrifice

They begin to tolerate discomfort without disappearing. They begin to choose relationships where effort flows both ways.

# Chapter 18

## Marriage as the Breaking Point
*Why Commitment Can Reactivate Old Wounds*


Marriage is often imagined as a place of stability, a promise that love will stay. For many people, commitment brings comfort, structure, and belonging. But for those who experienced early separation or abandonment, marriage can become something else entirely. It can act as a mirror, reflecting wounds that were never fully healed.

This does not happen because the marriage is unhealthy or because the partner is unsafe. It happens because commitment changes the emotional landscape. It asks the nervous system to trust permanence, intimacy, and reliance on another person. For someone, whose early experience taught them that bonds can disappear, this request alone can be activating.

Marriage does not create the wound. It exposes what was already there.

### When Commitment Feels Like Risk

In long-term relationships partners become emotionally central. Decisions are shared. Futures are planned. Marriage brings emotional reliance, shared responsibilities, and, in some cases, financial dependence. For individuals with unresolved abandonment, this level of closeness can trigger a deep internal alarm.

The nervous system may interpret commitment not as safety, but as vulnerability.

Thoughts that surface are often subtle but persistent.

What happens if this relationship falls apart?
What if I am left again?

These fears are not conscious choices. They are survival memories resurfacing in a new context.

**Who the Abandoned Child Often Attracts**

People with abandonment histories are often drawn to partners who feel familiar at a nervous-system level. This does not mean unhealthy relationships are chosen intentionally. It means the body gravitates toward emotional patterns it recognizes.

Often, the abandoned child attracts partners who are emotionally intense, deeply bonded early on, or themselves fearful of loss. These relationships can feel powerful at the start, fast, meaningful, and consuming. The connection feels real, urgent, and deeply affirming.

This intensity is often mistaken for security but in reality, it is mutual activation. Familiar emotional patterns can feel safer than unfamiliar stability, even when they bring volatility with them.

**When Both Partners Carry Abandonment Wounds**

When two people with abandonment histories marry, the bond can feel especially strong and especially fragile.

Both partners may fear being left.
Both may fear being too much.
Both may find it hard to trust that love will stay when the relationship becomes permanent.

In the beginning, this can look like devotion and closeness. Each partner feels seen in ways they never were before. But over time, the same wounds that drew them together begin to surface.

One partner may cling while the other withdraws.
Both may cling, creating emotional intensity that leaves little room for anyone else.
Small conflicts may feel catastrophic.
Distance may feel like danger. The marriage becomes the emotional lifeline.

Why Marriage Can Shift Old Loyalties

As a committed relationship deepens, loyalty naturally reorganizes. A spouse becomes the primary emotional attachment. This shift is healthy, but for someone with abandonment history, it can feel destabilizing.

To manage this discomfort, some people unconsciously redirec attachment energy in ways that narrow their world.

They may over-invest emotionally in the spouse while pulling away from extended family.
They may idealize biological parents who were absent.
They may rewrite family narratives to make the present attachment feel safer.
They may create emotional boundaries that look more like withdrawal than balance.

In these moments, the family who once provided care may begin to feel moved to the background or even threatening, no because they did anything wrong, but because they are associated with earlier vulnerability.

How the Family Who Stayed Can Become the Silent Casualty

Families who stepped in during abandonment often expect that bond to remain permanent. They remember the sacrifices, the years of care, the role they played in keeping the child safe. When distance grows after marriage, they may feel confused, rejected, or replaced.

From the outside, it can look like ingratitude or emotional abandonment in reverse.

From the inside, something very different is happening.

Marriage has activated the original attachment wound, and the nervous system is protecting itself by narrowing focus. The spouse becomes the anchor. Everyone else, especially those connected to the original separation, may be unconsciously pushed to the margins.

The nervous system becomes highly alert. It scans for anything connected to earlier vulnerability. The family who stayed becomes emotionally linked to that chapter of life, even if they were not the cause of the loss.

The nervous system isn't asking:

- Who caused this?

- Who loved me?

- Who protected me?

It's asking:

- Where was I when this happened?

- Who was around when I felt powerless?

- What reminds me of that feeling?

**When Attachment Turns Into Isolation**

In some marriages, attachment becomes intense and exclusive. The individual may rely heavily on their spouse for emotional regulation, reassurance, and identity. When both partners carry abandonment wounds, this pattern can intensify.

This can lead to reduced contact with extended family, diminished emotional openness outside the marriage, defensiveness when family concerns are raised, and a belief that closeness to others threatens the marital bond.

Ironically, what began as a longing for connection can result in isolation.

The family who once served as a bridge during abandonment may now feel shut out not because they are no longer valued, but because the nervous system is guarding against loss.

The nervous system isn't asking:
- Who caused this?
- Who loved me?
- Who protected me?

It's asking:
- Where was I when this happened?
- Who was around when I felt powerless?
- What reminds me of that feeling?

**The Idealization Trap**

Another dynamic may emerge after marriage: the idealization of absent biological parents. Commitment often reawakens questions of origin, identity, and belonging. A spouse can become a safe container for these longings, unintentionally encouraging emotional distance from the family who raised the individual.

In some cases, the biological parent becomes emotionally elevated in the mind. Their absence is reframed as misunderstood or justified. The family who stayed is quietly devalued to make space for this ideal.

This shift is rarely intentional. It is an attempt to reconcile unfinished attachment within a new bond.

Real Challenges Inside the Marriage

Partners may begin to notice sudden emotional withdrawal after marriage, resistance to family involvement, anxiety around holidays or milestones, strong reactions to perceived rejection, and ongoing conflict around loyalty and boundaries.

## What Healing Requires in Committed Relationships

Healing does not require choosing a spouse over family, or family over spouse. It requires awareness.

Awareness that commitment can reactivate old wounds. Awareness that withdrawal is often fear, not rejection. Awareness that attachment history shapes present behavior. Awareness that loyalty shifts are natural, but isolation is not.

Healthy attachment allows for both: a primary bond with a spouse and meaningful connection with family.

## Reconnecting Without Reopening the Wound

For individuals with abandonment history, healing involves learning that closeness does not require removal. Marriage does not need to replace earlier bonds; it can coexist with both of them.

For families who stayed, healing may involve recognizing that distance after marriage is not always personal rejection. It is often a sign that something old has been stirred.

For partners, healing begins with curiosity rather than blame, and with the understanding that fear, once named, no longer needs to run the relationship.

# Chapter 19

## Naming the Loss Without Assigning Blame
*Healing Without Villains*

For many people, healing feels impossible without someone to blame.

Pain demands an explanation. Loss demands a cause. And when something hurts deeply, especially in childhood, the mind searches for a villain, someone whose failure can make the suffering feel justified and real.

But not all wounds are caused by cruelty.
Not all losses have a perpetrator.
And not all healing requires an enemy.

This chapter is about learning to name what was lost without turning someone into the reason it hurt.

### Why Blame Can Feel Necessary

Blame offers structure. It gives pain a place to land.

When loss feels confusing or unresolved, blame can bring temporary relief. It answers the question Why did this happen to me? with a sense of certainty. Someone failed. Someone chose wrong. Someone could have done better.

For many survivors, this feels safer than sitting with uncertainty.

But blame also narrows the story. It simplifies what was complex. It replaces grief with anger and replaces vulnerability with control. While this can feel stabilizing at first, it often keeps healing out of reach.

### The Difference Between Responsibility and Blame

Naming loss does not require assigning fault.

Responsibility acknowledges impact. Blame assigns intention.

A caregiver can be responsible for a rupture without meaning harm. A system can fail without malicious intent. Circumstance can overwhelm without anyone choosing to cause pain.

Healing requires honesty about what happened, not judgment about why.

### Why Villains Can Stall Healing

When healing depends on blame, it becomes conditional.

If someone must admit fault before the pain is valid, the survivor remains stuck waiting for acknowledgment that may never come. If healing requires condemnation, peace remains out of reach.

Villains keep the focus outside the self.

Grief, however, lives inside.

### What Naming the Loss Actually Looks Like

Naming the loss means saying, clearly and without apology:

- Something important was interrupted.
- Something I needed was missing.
- This affected me, even if no one intended it.

This kind of naming does not erase love, sacrifice, or effort. It simply allows the full truth to exist.

Care can be real. Loss can be real. Both can be true.

## Why This Is So Difficult

Many survivors fear that naming loss without blame will invalidate their pain. They worry it will sound like minimizing or excusing what happened.

In reality, the opposite is true.

Blame focuses outward.
Naming loss brings the experience inward where healing happens.

It allows grief to be felt without justification. It allows pain to exist without argument.

## What Healing Without Villains Makes Possible

When blame is released, something softens.

Relationships become more honest.
Memories become less rigid.
The nervous system no longer needs to defend its pain.

This does not mean reconciliation is required. It does not mean harm is denied. It means healing is no longer dependent on someone else being wrong.

## A Different Kind of Strength

Healing without villains requires courage.

It asks the survivor to sit with complexity. To hold grief without rage. To accept that some pain has no clean explanation.

But it also offers freedom.

Freedom from carrying anger that no longer serves.
Freedom from rewriting the past to justify the present. Freedom to heal on one's own terms.

# Chapter 20

## A Father's Letter to His Adult Child

My dear child,

I want to speak to you honestly, as your father.

I didn't grow up with a father who showed me how to be emotionally present. I learned how to work, how to provide, how to endure but not how to express warmth, comfort, or vulnerability in the way a child needs. For a long time, I truly believed that showing up, paying the bills, and keeping you safe meant I was doing what a good father should do.

I see now that love has more than one language.

I loved you in the only way I knew how, but not always in the way you needed to receive it. And that is something I take responsibility for.

I understand now that being physically present is not the same as being emotionally available. I understand that my focus on responsibility, stability, and survival may have made me seem distant or unreachable at times. I never meant to make you feel unseen, but I can see now how that may have happened.

If I could go back, I would slow down.
I would listen more instead of assuming I understood. I would ask how you were feeling instead of expecting you to be strong. I would make space for your emotions, even when I didn't know how to respond to them.
I would choose connection more often, not just duty.

I know now that love is not only shown through sacrifice. It is felt through presence.

I also want you to know this: I didn't withhold love because I didn't care. I withheld what I never learned how to give. That does not erase the impact, but it explains the gap.

I am not writing this to ask for forgiveness or to rewrite the past. I am writing because I see you more clearly now than I did before. I see how my limitations may have shaped your experience, and I want to take responsibility for that.

If you allow it, I want the chance to show up differently now. Not as the father who believes he has all the answers, but as one who is willing to listen, learn, and grow.

If you need space, I will respect that.
If you are not ready, I will understand.
My hope is not to undo the past, but to be accountable in the present.

No matter what you choose, I want you to know this:

You mattered.
Your feelings were real.
And it was my responsibility to see you.

With humility and love,


**Dad**

# Chapter 21

## When Awareness Is Not Enough
*Why Understanding the Wound Does Not Automatically Heal It*

Awareness is often celebrated as the turning point, the momen everything is supposed to change. The day you finally name what happened. The day you recognize the wound. The day th the past stops being a fog and find its words.

But for many survivors, awareness is not the end of suffering. is the beginning of a deeper reckoning.

There is a quiet betrayal that follows insight when pain does no immediately loosen its grip. You read the books. You connect the dots. You understand *why* you became who you became. And still, your body flinches. Your heart overreacts. Your relationships strain under patterns you swear you see clearly now.

This is where many people begin to doubt themselves.
If I understand it, why am I still affected? If
I can explain it, why does it still hurt?

Because awareness illuminates the wound, but it does not close it.

Understanding is cognitive. Healing is embodied. And the two do not move at the same speed.

For years, survival required adaptation. Your nervous system learned how to stay alert, how to anticipate loss, how to read rooms for danger, how to shrink or over-extend to keep connection intact. These responses were not choices; they wer necessities. They were rehearsed thousands of times before yo ever had words for them.

Insight does not erase conditioning.
Language does not undo muscle memory.
Clarity does not automatically calm a body trained for threat.

You may know that you are safe now, yet your chest tightens anyway.
You may recognize that a reaction is disproportionate, yet it still arrives with force.
You may intellectually trust someone, yet your body braces for abandonment before your mind can intervene.

This is not failure.
This is the residue of survival.

Awareness can feel cruel because it removes the mystery but leaves the pain intact. Before, you suffered without explanation. Now, you suffer with one, and that can feel even heavier. There is grief in realizing how long you lived in adaptation. There is anger in seeing how much of your life was shaped by something you never consented to. There is exhaustion in recognizing patterns without yet having the capacity to stop them.

Healing does not happen at the speed of understanding because the wound was not created through understanding. It was created through repetition, powerlessness, and unmet needs over time. It lives in the nervous system, not just the mind.

This is why awareness alone can become another burden. Survivors begin to shame themselves for still struggling. They weaponize insight against their own humanity.
I should know better.
I'm self-aware why am I still like this?

But healing is not an intellectual achievement. It is a process of retraining safety. It requires patience, repetition, and compassion that does not demand immediate transformation.

Awareness is the map.
Healing is the journey.
And no one walks a long road in a single step.

There will be moments when you react before you realize why. Moments when old behaviors surface despite your best intentions. Moments when growth feels invisible. This does not mean awareness has failed you. It means awareness has done its job, by telling the truth, and now something deeper is required.

What heals is not knowing what happened.
What heals is learning how to stay present when your body wants to flee.
What heals is practicing safety long after danger has passed.
What heals is allowing progress to be slow without calling it regression.

Reclamation is not about becoming untriggered. It is about becoming less afraid of your own responses. It is about meeting yourself with understanding and patience. It is about honoring the part of you that learned to survive and teaching it, gently, that survival is no longer the only option

## Chapter 22

## When Parenthood Reopens the Wound
*Why the Questions Arrive and What They Are Really Asking*

For many survivors of early separation or emotional loss, life moves forward without much reflection on the past.

They build careers.

Form relationships.

Create routines.

They learn how to function. Some even believe they have healed.

And then they become parents.

This is often the moment when questions rise quietly at first, then with increasing urgency.

Not casual questions. Not intellectual ones.

But deeply personal questions that emerge from the body before the mind has time to interpret them.

What made you say yes?
What did you have to tell yourself to leave?
How did you live with that decision?
Why don't I remember the goodbye?
Why does this suddenly start to hurt?

These questions do not surface because something is wrong. They surface because something long held inside is finally ready to be felt.

## Why Parenthood Reopens the Past

Becoming a parent shifts perspective in a profound way.

For the first time, the survivor is no longer only the child in the story.
They now stand in the role their caregiver once held.

This changes everything.

Suddenly, the meaning of presence becomes real.
The weight of responsibility becomes tangible.
The instinct to stay, protect, and sacrifice becomes embodied.

And with that comes a reckoning.

What once felt abstract now feels personal.
What once felt excusable now carries emotional weight.

The survivor is no longer asking questions as a child. They are asking them as someone who understands what it means to care.

That is when the nervous system begins to stir.


## Why These Questions Feel So Urgent

The nervous system does not seek answers out of curiosity. It seeks resolution.

When separation happens early, the child's mind cannot process motive, context, or limitation. The body simply records loss. That loss is stored without explanation.

But when the survivor becomes a parent, the body now has new information.

It understands:
• how difficult leaving would be

- how instinctive protection feels
- how powerful attachment becomes

This creates a collision between past and present.

The survivor is holding two truths at once:

- I was left.
- I would not leave.

The brain tries to reconcile the difference.

And that reconciliation often sounds like questions.

**"What Made You Say Yes?"**

This question is not about logistics.

It is about meaning.

It asks:
What made you choose a path that did not include me?
What made that choice survivable?
Where did I fall in that decision?

Beneath the question is a deeper longing:

**What made our time together something you couldn't continue?**

This is not accusation.
It is an attempt to locate oneself in the story not as an afterthought, but as someone whose presence mattered.

**"What Did You Have to Tell Yourself to Leave?"**

This question reflects emotional intelligence, not anger.

Most people cannot walk away from a child without creating a narrative that makes the decision bearable. The survivor senses this.

They are asking:
What did you have to believe to survive that moment?

Did you convince yourself I would be okay?
Did you have to shut something down to go on?

This question often emerges when the survivor realizes how devastating such a choice would feel to them now.

It is the mind trying to understand how something so painful could have been endured.

**"What Made It Emotionally Possible?"**

This question comes from the realization that love and loss can coexist.

The survivor wonders:
How did you keep going afterward?
Did you feel pain the way I do now?
Did you grieve me or did you have to stop feeling altogether?

Often, this question arises when the survivor recognizes their own emotional depth and wonders how someone else survived such a rupture.

The underlying fear is quiet but powerful:
If I would have been shattered by this, what does it mean that you weren't shattered?

**"Why Don't I Remember the Goodbye?"**

This question carries the most grief.

And the answer is rooted in neuroscience.

When loss occurs early or under overwhelming conditions, the brain may not store it as narrative memory. Instead, it stores it as sensation.

The body remembers:
• the separation
• the shock
• the emotional rupture

But the mind does not hold images, words, or sequence.

This is not repression. It
is protection.

The absence of memory does not mean nothing happened.
It means what happened was too much to process at the time.

The memory lives in the nervous system, not the story.


## Why These Questions Often Appear After Becoming a Parent

Parenthood activates attachment circuitry.

It awakens empathy.
It deepens understanding.
It clarifies what it means to stay.

Suddenly, the survivor understands what their caregiver may not have been able to give.

And that understanding brings grief.

Not blame.
Not judgment.

Grief.

Because now the survivor sees clearly:

* how vulnerable they once were
* how much they needed
* how little explanation they received

This is not regression.
It is maturation.

## What the Survivor Is Really Grieving

At the heart of these questions is not

anger.

It is grief for:
* the absence of explanation
* the lack of emotional continuity
* the feeling of being chosen without condition • the chance to
  understand what happened in real time

The survivor is not longing for the past.
They are grieving, what was never available to them when it
mattered most.

## Why This Stage Feels So Intense

This phase can feel overwhelming because it is the first time the
grief is conscious.

**As a child:**
* you adapted
* you survived
* you moved forward
**As an adult:**
* you understand
* you feel
* you integrate

That shift can be painful.

But it is also a sign of healing.

If you are asking these questions now, nothing is wrong with you.

You are not reopening a wound.
You are finally allowing it to close correctly.

You are not regressing. You are integrating.

And the fact that these questions are arising now means something important:

You survived what once overwhelmed you.

And now, at last, your nervous system is ready to understand it.

# Chapter 23.

## Separating the Wound From the Self
*You Are Not the Story That Hurt You*

For many people who grew up with abandonment or early emotional loss, the wound does not simply exist inside them, it becomes them.

They don't just carry pain; they organize their identity around it. They don't just remember what happened; they unconsciously become what happened.

This is not weakness.
It is what happens when pain arrives before language, before choice, before the self has fully formed.

When abandonment occurs early, there is no solid sense of identity yet. There is no "me" separate from experience. So the nervous system does the only thing it can do, it builds the self around what happened in order to survive it.

This chapter is about separating who you are from what you lived through.

Not by denying the wound.
Not by minimizing it.
But by finally understanding that the wound is something you carry, not something you are.

## How Abandonment Becomes an Identity

When loss happens early, the mind does not say:
"This is an experience I am having."

It says:
"This is who I am."

Children do not yet have the ability to contextualize events. They cannot say:
"My parent left because of their own limitations."
"My environment changed for reasons outside my control."
"This pain is temporary."

Instead, they personalize the experience.

They form conclusions like:
• I am too much.
• I am not enough.
• People leave.
• I have to earn love.
• I must not need too much.

Over time, these conclusions stop feeling like beliefs and start feeling like identity.

The wound becomes the lens through which everything is interpreted.

This is why many adults don't say:
"I experienced abandonment."

They say:
"I am unlovable."
"I'm difficult."
"I'm too much."
"I don't belong."

The injury becomes the identity.

## Why Self-Blame Feels Safer

One of the most painful truths in psychology is this:

The mind would rather blame itself than accept that loss can b
random. Self-blame gives the illusion of control.

If *I* caused it, then *I* can prevent it from happening again.
If *I* was the problem, then *I* can fix myself.
If *I* wasn't enough, then maybe next time I will be.

This belief system feels safer than the alternative:
That something painful happened for reasons beyond your
control.

For a child, believing "it was my fault" is less terrifying than
believing:
"I had no power, and it could happen again."

So the child chooses the story that allows survival.

That story often follows them into adulthood.


## When the Wound Becomes the Personality

Over time, survival strategies solidify into identity traits.

A child who learned to disappear becomes an adult who
minimizes their needs.

A child who learned to perform becomes an adult who
overachieves and over gives.

A child who learned not to rely on others becomes
hyper=independent.

A child who learned that connection disappears becomes
hypervigilant in relationships.

These are adaptations.

But when they go unexamined, they quietly run a person's life.

The danger is not in having these traits.
The danger is believing they define who you are.

## Narrative Therapy: Rewriting the Story Without Erasing the Truth

Narrative psychology teaches that healing begins when we separate the person from the problem.

Not: "I am
broken."

But:
"I learned to survive something painful."

Not:
"I am too much."

But:
"I adapted to instability by becoming alert and responsive."

Not:
"This is who I am."

But:
"This is what happened to me." This

shift is subtle, but profound.

It allows the nervous system to relax.
It creates space for self-compassion.
It opens the door to change without shame.

You are not erasing your past.

You are seeing it with the understanding you didn't have when you were living it.

**Internal Family Systems: Understanding the Parts of You**

Internal Family Systems (IFS) offers a powerful lens here.

It explains that the self is made up of "parts," emotional states that formed to protect you.

Some parts learned to:
• Please
• Perform
• Detach
• Control
• Stay quiet
• Stay strong

These are strategies that once kept you safe.

When abandonment occurs, certain parts become overdeveloped because they had to be.

But healing happens when you realize:
You are not the protector.
You are not the frightened child. You are not the wound.

You are the one who has these parts.

And that distinction matters.


**Learning to Say: "This Happened to Me"**

One of the most powerful moments in healing is when the language changes.

From:

"This is just how I am."

To:
"This is something that happened to me."

That shift creates space.

It allows grief without self-condemnation.
It allows compassion without weakness. It
allows growth without erasure.

You can honor what you survived without living inside it.

**Building a Self Beyond Survival**

When identity has been shaped by survival, safety can feel
unfamiliar.

Some people feel lost when they are no longer struggling.
Some feel empty when they stop performing.
Some feel anxious when there is no crisis to manage.

This is not because something is wrong.

It is because survival used to give life structure.

Healing invites something new: choice.

Who are you when you're not bracing?
Who are you when you're not proving?
Who are you when you don't have to earn belonging?

These questions can feel unsettling, but they are the beginning
of freedom.

# Chapter 24.

## Honoring the Survival Strategies Without Living Inside Them

*What Saved You Then Is Not What Will Sustain You Now*

Survival strategies are not character flaws. They are the ways your nervous system learned to keep you connected, protected, and steady when connection felt uncertain. Over giving, appeasing, hyper-independence, perfectionism, these were not random habits. They were intelligent responses to an environment where safety wasn't guaranteed.

But what protected you then can begin to cost you now.

Healing is not about getting rid of these strategies with shame. It's about updating them with choice, so you can stay connected without disappearing and stay strong without staying alone.

### Step 1: Decide What You Want Now

**Not what you needed then. What you want today.**

Survival keeps you focused on avoiding pain. Healing shifts you into building the kind of life you actually want to live.

Ask yourself:

- What kind of connection do I want now?
- What feels safe today, emotionally, and relationally?
- What feels draining or forced?
- What do I no longer want to carry?

This step matters because your nervous system will keep using old strategies until you give it a new goal.

## Step 2: Change Expectations Before You Change Relationships

Many survivors try to heal by doing something external first—explaining, confronting, distancing, or cutting someone off.

But relief doesn't come from changing the relationship first. Relief comes from changing the hope attached to it.

Before you decide how close to remain, how much to share, or what boundaries you need, get honest about this:

- What am I still hoping this person will one day give me?
- What reaction or recognition am I waiting for?
- For what "repair moment" do I keep returning?

When expectations are out of alignment with reality, even small interactions can feel sharp. A short response feels like rejection. A neutral comment feels like dismissal. Silence feels like being left again.

Changing expectations is not lowering your standards.
It's placing your emotional weight where it can actually be held.

## Step 3: Stop Bringing Vulnerable Needs to Unsafe Places

This is one of the most powerful shifts a survivor can make, not dramatic, not loud, but deeply stabilizing.

"Unsafe" does **not** mean abusive.
It means not able to hold emotional truth without minimizing, deflecting, or shutting down.

### What this looks like in real life

**Scenario: The parent who provides but can't attune** An adult child shares: "I felt lonely growing up. I needed more emotional connection."

The parent responds: "You had everything you needed. I worked hard. You were taken care of."

Nothing cruel is said. But the emotional door closes.
The adult child leaves feeling guilty for even speaking.

The problem is not that the adult child is asking for something unreasonable.
The problem is that this parent can offer **provision**, but not **emotional presence** in hard conversations.

So the healing move is not "try again, explain better." The healing move is for individuals to choose a different place for that level of vulnerability.

**Step 4: Learn to Protect Your Energy Without Cutting People Off**

A lot of survivors think the only options are overexpose or disappear.

There's a healthier middle: stay connected with clarity.

What this looks like in real life

**Scenario: staying in contact without reopening wounds**
You still call your parent. You still visit. You still show respect. But you stop bringing your most tender emotional needs into that relationship.

Instead, you shift how you engage:

- You keep emotionally charged topics limited

- You choose neutral or present-day subjects when needed

- You end conversations early when you feel yourself getting overwhelmed

- You stop trying to "prove" your experience

You share your deepest emotions with safer people (or in private reflection)

This is emotional protection.

## Step 5: Limit Emotionally Charged Conversations

Limiting isn't avoidance. It's knowing what tends to spiral you and choosing not to step into that fire.

### Example

If every attempt to discuss your pain ends in defensiveness, minimizing, or argument, you don't keep returning to that conversation hoping the outcome will suddenly be different.

You practice a simple exit line:

- "I don't want to discuss this right now."

- "This conversation isn't feeling productive for me."

- "I'm going to stop here."

No long explanation. No debate. Just a clean pause.

This protects your nervous system from repeated injury.

## Step 6: Avoid Sharing Vulnerable Details With Unsafe Listeners

Not everyone earns access to your inner world.

**Example**

You share something tender with someone and afterward you feel:

- exposed
- ashamed
- confused
- regretful
- emotionally worse

That's information.

Next time, you share less, not because you're shutting down, but because you're choosing your emotional container wisely.

A safe listener doesn't have to agree with everything.
They just don't punish you for feeling.

**Step 7: Reduce Emotional Reactivity**

Reactivity is when your body responds to the present as if it's the past.

The goal isn't to become numb.
The goal is to build a pause between trigger and response.

**What this looks like**

You notice the first body signal, tight chest, heat, urgency, the urge to defend or overexplain.

Then you delay action by 60 seconds.

- breathe
- step away
- get water
- write one sentence in your phone: "I feel activated. I can respond later."

That pause is how you stop survival from driving the conversation.

**Step 8: Practice Repair Only Where It's Possible**

Repair is possible when the other person can listen without defensiveness

- acknowledge impact without arguing intention stay regulated during discomfort respect your emotional limits

If those conditions aren't present, don't chase repair there. Choose closure instead of confrontation.

Closure is internal.
It's the moment you stop auditioning your pain for someone who can't hold it.

**Step 9: Replace Survival With Choice**

This is the whole point of the chapter.

You don't have to stop being loving.
You stop loving in ways that erase you.

You begin practicing:

- pausing instead of over-functioning
- asking instead of assuming
- leaving conversations instead of enduring them
- receiving support without earning it first

## Chapter 25

## How to Protect Yourself Without Cutting People Off
*Boundaries Without Panic*

For many survivors, the word *boundary* feels intimidating.

It sounds harsh.
Final.

Some imagine it means confrontation, conflict, or walking away from people they still care about. Others fear that setting boundaries will make them selfish, cold, or ungrateful.

But boundaries are not walls.
They are clarity.

They are not about controlling others.
They are about regulating yourself.

This chapter is about learning how to create emotional safety without shutting down, cutting people off, or reliving old wounds. It is about learning how to stay connected without abandoning yourself.

### Why Boundaries Feel So Hard for Survivors

If you grew up with emotional inconsistency, boundaries often feel dangerous.

Many survivors learned early that:

- Needs created tension

  Feelings caused discomfort
  Speaking up led to withdrawal or conflict
  Staying quiet preserved connection

So the nervous system learned an equation: Connection =

Compliance

That belief doesn't disappear just because you grow up. It shows up later as:

- Over-explaining
- Avoiding conflict
- Saying yes when you mean no
- Feeling guilty for needing space
- Staying in conversations that hurt

Boundaries feel threatening because, once upon a time, losing connection was a real danger.

But boundaries are not about

rejection. They are about regulation.

**What Boundaries Actually Are**

A boundary is not a demand.

A boundary is a decision you make about:

- What you will engage in
- What you will step back from
- How much emotional access someone has
- What you do when a limit is crossed

It does **not** require:

- Explaining yourself repeatedly
- Convincing the other person
- Getting permission
- Proving your reasons

A boundary is something you *live*, not something you argue.

## Step #1: Start With Expectations, Not Behavior

Most people try to change relationships by changing behavior first:

- Saying less
- Pulling away
- Confronting
- Explaining

But real change begins with expectations.

Ask yourself:

- What do I expect this person to give emotionally?
- What do I keep hoping will be different?
- What am I waiting for them to understand?

If your expectations exceed someone's emotional capacity, pain is inevitable.

This is not about blame.
It is about accuracy.

When expectations shift, emotional reactions soften.

## Step #2: Learn the Difference Between Safe and Unsafe Emotional Spaces

An emotionally safe person:

- Listens without rushing to fix
- Does not argue with your feelings
- Allows discomfort without becoming defensive
- Leaves you feeling calmer afterward An emotionally unsafe person:

Minimizes your feelings
Becomes irritated or defensive
Explains you away

- Makes you feel dramatic or ungrateful
- Leaves you feeling smaller or confused This distinction is essential.

You do not need to stop loving people who are emotionally unsafe.

You *do* need to stop bringing your most vulnerable parts to them.

**Step #3: Practice Boundaries Without Announcing Them**

Boundaries do not require speeches.
Most effective boundaries are quiet.

**Example 1:**
Instead of:
"I need you to understand how much this hurt me."
You shift to:
"I'm not going to talk about this right now."

**Example 2:**
Instead of:
"Why can't you ever listen to me?"
You choose:
"I'll talk about this with someone who can hold it."

**Example 3:**
Instead of:
"I just want you to see me."
You decide:
"I won't seek emotional reassurance here anymore."

This is not avoidance.
It is discernment.

## Step #4: Learn to Tolerate the Discomfort of Boundaries

Boundaries often bring guilt before they bring peace. You may feel:

- Selfish
- Cold
- Afraid of hurting someone
- Afraid of being misunderstood
- Tempted to explain or take it back
- This is normal.

Your nervous system is adjusting to a new pattern: **Choosing yourself without apology.**

The discomfort does not mean the boundary is wrong. It means the pattern is changing.

## Step#5: Reduce Emotional Reactivity

When boundaries are weak, emotions tend to spike. When boundaries strengthen, reactivity softens. Reducing emotional reactivity means:

- Pausing before responding
- Not explaining when you feel flooded
- Taking space before reacting
- Letting intensity pass before speaking Instead of

"I have to fix this now."

You learn:

"I can respond when I'm grounded."

This is not withdrawal.

It is regulation.

## Step#6: Know When Repair Is Possible and When It Isn't

Repair is only possible if the other person can:

- Listen without defensiveness
- Acknowledge impact

- Stay emotionally present
- Respect your limits

If those qualities are absent, the work shifts inward.
You stop trying to be understood.
You start protecting your peace.

This is not giving up.
It is choosing reality over hope that keeps hurting.

## Step#7: Grieve What Will Not Change

You grieve:

- The parent who couldn't show up emotionally
- The relationship you wished you had
- The conversations that never happened
- The safety you needed but didn't receive

This grief is not anger. It is honesty.

And it creates freedom.

Because once you stop hoping someone will change,
you stop reopening the wound.

## What Healthy Boundaries Look Like in Real Life

- You stop over-explaining
- You share selectively
- You leave conversations sooner
- You feel less emotionally drained
- You trust your reactions more
- You feel calmer after interactions
- You no longer need to prove your pain:

You stop asking others to validate what you already know.

## A Grounding Truth to Carry Forward

Boundaries are not about pushing people away.

They are about staying close to yourself.

You are allowed to protect your emotional energy.
You are allowed to choose where your vulnerability goes.
You are allowed to stop explaining your pain.

And you are allowed to build relationships that feel safe, not because you endured them, but because they allow you to be fully present.

# Chapter 26:

## A Letter from a Son Who Was Left Behind:

Mom,

I've spent a long time trying to understand what happened when you left. As a kid, I didn't have the words for it. I only knew that one day you were there, and then you weren't there, nothing was ever the same after that.

I want you to know something I never said aloud: I thought it was my fault.

I wondered if I had done something wrong. If I wasn't good enough. If I had been quieter, better behaved, easier to love, maybe you would have stayed. When you're a child and someone leaves, you don't think, *They had their own reasons*. You think *I must not have been worth staying for*.

I needed you. I needed your voice, your comfort, your reassurance. I needed to know that I mattered to you, that I was still important even when life got hard. Instead, I learned how to be strong too early. I learned how to hide what I felt. I learned how to pretend I didn't need anyone.

But the truth is, I did.

I needed you to tell me you were proud of me. I needed to hear that I was doing okay. I needed to know that my mistakes didn't make me unlovable. I needed you to check on me, to ask how I was really doing, to notice when I was hurting even if I didn't say it out loud.

When you left, the silence spoke louder than any words ever could.

I grew up carrying questions I never got answers to. I carried anger I didn't understand. I carried a sadness I couldn't explain And for a long time, I carried it alone.

I'm not writing this to blame you. I'm writing it because I'm finally trying to heal. I'm trying to make sense of the part of me that still wonders why I wasn't enough to make you stay. I'm trying to learn that your leaving was about your pain, your limits, your story not my worth.

I want you to know that I survived. I grew. I kept going. But a part of me will always be the boy who waited, who hoped, who needed his mother and didn't know how to say it.

This letter is not an accusation.
It's an acknowledgment:
Of what was missing
Of what mattered
Of what still echoes

Your Son

# Chapter 27

## Understanding the Parent's Experience Without Blame
*The pain of grieving you the loss of your child who is alive*


This section is written for parents.

Not to accuse.
Not to dissect mistakes.
Not to assign fault.

But to name something that many parents carry quietly and often alone: the pain of doing everything you knew how to do and still feeling a distance you cannot explain.

Many parents look back and say:

"I was there."
"I worked hard."
"I provided."
"I sacrificed." "I did
the best I could."

And all of that may be true.

Yet years later, when an adult child expresses pain, distance, or emotional absence, parents are often left stunned. Confused. Hurt. Sometimes defensive. Often heartbroken.

Because from the parent's perspective, love was never missing.

So how does this happen?

## When Love Is Expressed Through Survival

Many parents raised children during periods of intense stress, financial pressure, generational trauma, immigration, single parenting, illness, emotional isolation, or lack of support.

For these parents, love was not something discussed.
It was something done.

Love looked like:
• Working long hours
• Paying bills
• Keeping the household afloat
• Protecting children from hardship
• Pushing through exhaustion
• Suppressing personal needs

In many families, especially those shaped by scarcity or hardship, emotional expression was a luxury. Survival came first

Parents learned:
"I show love by providing."
"I stay strong, so my children don't have to worry."
"My feelings don't matter as long as they're okay."

And for many years, this worked.

But emotional connection requires more than provision.
It requires presence, availability, things that are difficult to offer when a parent is overwhelmed, unsupported, or carrying unresolved pain of their own.

## Why Parents Often Don't See the Disconnect

Most parents did not intentionally withhold connection.

They were:
• Exhausted

- Overworked
- Emotionally under-supported
- Raised without emotional modeling
- Taught to suppress their own needs

When a child became quiet, independent, or complaining, it was often interpreted as maturity.

Not distress.

When a child stopped asking for attention, it was often seen as growth.

Not adaptation.

And because the child was functioning, going to school, behaving, meeting expectations, there were few external signs that something was missing.

From the parent's perspective:
"There were no problems."
"We were doing okay."
"They never said anything."

But children rarely have the words to explain emotional absence. They communicate through behavior, not language.

**Why Parents and Children Remember the Same Home Differently**

This is one of the most painful realities for families to confront.

Parents remember:
- What they provided
- What they sacrificed

- How hard they tried
- How much pressure they carried

Children remember:
• How often they felt alone
• How safe it felt to express emotions
• Whether they were comforted when overwhelmed • Whether their feelings were welcomed or minimized

Both experiences can be true at the same time.

This is not about one person being right and the other wrong. It is about two different nervous systems living in the same environment and interpreting it differently.

## When Parents Themselves Were Never Emotionally Held

Many parents were raised in homes where:
• Emotions were dismissed
• Vulnerability was unsafe
• Strength meant silence
• Needs were considered weakness

They were taught to endure, not express.

So when their own child needed emotional presence, they often had nothing internal to draw from. Not because they didn't care, but because they were never taught how.

This creates a quiet cycle:
A parent gives what they had.
A child needs what the parent never received.
Both feel unseen.

## Why This Can Lead to Distance Later in Life

As children grow into adults, something subtle but profound begins to happen. With maturity comes perspective. Experiences that once felt confusing or invisible start to take shape. The emotional gaps they couldn't name as children slowly come into focus, not as accusations, but as realizations.

This shift often surprises both the child and the parent.

The adult child may not come with anger or confrontation. In fact, many don't come with words at all. Instead, the change shows up quietly:

They share less.
They keep conversations surface-level.
They stop turning to their parent for emotional support.
They become careful about what they reveal.
They create space without fully understanding why.

To the parent, this distance can feel abrupt and deeply painful.

"I did everything for them."
"I sacrificed so much."
"I don't understand why they're pulling away."
"Why does it feel like I failed?"

From the parent's point of view, the relationship looks unchanged. The history is the same. The love was real. The effort was constant. So the distance feels confusing, sometimes even unfair.

But what's happening is not rejection.

It is recognition.

As children mature, they develop emotional language they didn't have before. They begin to notice patterns. They reflect on how they learned to cope. They start to understand what they needed but couldn't ask for.

This awareness often doesn't come with blame. It comes with grief.

Grief for moments that felt lonely.
Grief for feelings that went unspoken.

Grief for comfort that was needed but never quite reached them.

And because this realization can be overwhelming, many adults instinctively create distance, not out of punishment, but out of self-protection.

They are not pulling away because they don't love their parent.

They are pulling away because closeness now activates something unresolved.

**The Emotional Mismatch**

This is where the idea of mismatch becomes important.

The parent's language of love may have been:
Providing.
Protecting.
Enduring.
Doing.

The child's language of need may have been:
Being seen.
Being comforted.
Being emotionally understood.
Being reassured.

Both are valid.
But they are not the same language.

When a child grows up without having their emotional language consistently spoken, they often learn to translate their needs in silence. They adapt. They become strong. They stop asking.

Years later, when they finally understand what they were missing, they may not know how to bridge that gap with the same people who unknowingly created it.

So distance becomes the compromise.

Not because love is gone, but because
emotional safety still feels uncertain.

**Why This Feels So Painful for Parents**

For many parents, this stage brings a unique kind of heartbreak.

They may think:
"I gave everything I had."
"I didn't know they felt this way."
"I would have done something different if I'd known."

And that is often true.

But the difficulty lies here:
children rarely know how to explain emotional absence while
they are still living inside it.

By the time they understand it, the family roles are already
formed.

This can make parents feel blindsided, as though a verdict has
been passed without their knowledge.

But this is not judgment.
It is delayed awareness.

**The Truth Beneath the Distance**

The distance that forms in adulthood is rarely about punishment
or rejection.

It is usually about regulation.

The adult child is learning how to protect themselves
emotionally in ways they didn't know how to do before.

They are not trying to erase the relationship.
They are trying to survive it in a new way.

And often, what looks like withdrawal is actually an attempt to maintain connection without reopening old wounds.

## A Gentle Reframe for Parents

If your child feels distant, it does not mean your love was meaningless.
It does not mean you failed.
It does not mean you were a bad parent.

It means there was a difference between what you gave and what they were able to receive at the time.

That difference does not make either of you wrong.

It simply means the relationship now needs a different kind of understanding, one that honors both effort and impact, both love and limitation.

And sometimes, that understanding is the bridge that brings closeness back in a new, more honest way.

## What Parents Often Carry Silently

Many parents carry guilt they cannot name.
Confusion they don't understand.
Defensiveness that hides grief.

They may think:
"I gave everything I had."
"I didn't know what else to do."
"I thought love was enough."

And in many ways, it was.
But love without emotional attunement can still leave a child feeling unseen.

This does not make the parent bad.
It makes them human.

## A Gentle Truth for Parents

Your child's pain does not erase your effort.
Their grief does not cancel your sacrifice.
Their questions do not mean you failed.

It means something important was missing and neither of you may have had the tools to name it at the time.

Understanding this is about compassion.
For your child.
And for yourself.

Because many parents did the best they could with what they were given.

And sometimes, healing begins not with defending the past, but with understanding it.

# Chapter 28

## When Love Is Invisible:
### *The Hidden Grief of Stepparents*

There is a grief that rarely gets named.

It doesn't fit neatly into categories.
It isn't recognized by society.
And it is often carried in silence.

It is the grief of the stepparent who loved deeply,
showed up consistently, tried to do everything
right, and still feels unseen, unchosen, or quietly
replaced.

This chapter exists to give language to that experience.
Not to assign fault.
Not to defend or accuse.
But to help both sides understand why this dynamic can hurt so
deeply.

Because step-parenting carries a unique emotional weight that
few people truly understand.

## The Fear No One Talks About

Many stepparents enter a family already afraid.

Not of the child,
but of the role.

They carry an unspoken fear:
"I don't want to be the wicked stepparent."
"I don't want to overstep."

"I don't want to be resented."

"I don't want to cause harm."

So they overcorrect.

They become:
 extra careful
extra patient
extra giving
extra flexible

They hold back discipline.
They suppress frustration.
They try to be endlessly understanding.

Not because they don't care,
but because they care too much.

They are trying to earn safety in a role that has no clear rules.

## When Overcompensation Becomes Invisible

Many stepparents respond to this fear by becoming emotionally smaller.

They avoid conflict.
They avoid correction.
They avoid setting firm boundaries.
They avoid showing disappointment.

They believe:
"If I'm easy, I won't be rejected."
"If I don't push, I'll be accepted."
"If I give more, I'll be loved."

But over time, this creates an unintended dynamic.

The stepparent becomes the one who:
• gives without asking

- absorbs without expressing
- sacrifices quietly
- stays emotionally careful

And because the child does not see the inner effort, the sacrifice becomes invisible.

## The Painful Misinterpretation

One of the most painful moments for a stepparent is realizing:

The child believes the biological parent loved their biological children more. That may be the case for some but in this case, am making reference to the one who share equally and love equally.

This often happens when the biological parent disciplines more directly.

From the child's perspective:
"They don't care enough to correct me."
"They don't expect something from me."
"They're more invested in your own child."

From the stepparent's perspective:
"I held back because I didn't want to hurt them."
"I didn't discipline because I was afraid to overstep."
"I loved them enough to stay careful."

Two completely different interpretations.
Both rooted in love.
Both misunderstood.

## Why This Hurts the Stepparent So Deeply

The pain cuts deeper because stepparents choose the relationship.

They were not obligated by biology.

They were not required by circumstance.
They chose to show up.

And when that effort goes unrecognized or worse,
misunderstood, it can feel devastating.

The grief sounds like:
"I gave everything I had."
"I tried so hard to do it right."
"I stayed when I didn't have to."
"Why wasn't that enough?"

This pain often remains unspoken because stepparents fear
sounding selfish or resentful.

So they carry it quietly.


**Why the Adult Child May Not See the Sacrifice**

From the child's side, the experience is very different.

Children don't measure love by effort.
They measure it by emotional clarity.

They often don't notice restraint.
They don't recognize self-control.
They don't understand the fear behind gentleness.

What they see is:
Who corrected me?
Who set limits?
Who showed authority?
Who seemed confident in their role?

And because the stepparent held back, the child may
interpret that as emotional distance rather than protection.

Not because the stepparent failed, but
because children cannot see intention.
They only feel impact.

## The Emotional Gap That Forms

This creates a painful gap:

The stepparent feels:
"I gave everything and still wasn't chosen."

The child feels:
"I never really knew where I stood."

Both experiences can coexist.
Neither is wrong.
Both are rooted in unmet emotional clarity.

And because neither side talks about it openly,
the distance grows quietly over time.

## Why This Hurts More Later in Life

As the child grows into adulthood, they begin forming their
own identity and relationships.

They pull away naturally.
They become less dependent.
They redirect emotional energy elsewhere.

For the stepparent, this can feel like loss layered on top of
silence.

Not only was the bond unclear,
now it feels gone.

And because the stepparent never felt fully entitled to
the relationship, they may feel they have no right to
grieve it.

That grief often becomes:
- confusion
- sadness
- resentment
- self-doubt
- or emotional withdrawal because they loved without assurance.

## A Truth That Holds Both Sides

Here is what matters most:

A stepparent can love deeply and still feel unseen.
A child can feel disconnected without intending harm.
A parent can act from fear rather than absence of love.
A relationship can suffer without anyone being wrong.

This is not about blame.
It is about misalignment.
About unspoken fears.
About roles that were never clearly defined.

## What Healing Looks Like Here

Healing does not require revisiting the past with accusations.

It begins with understanding:

- That restraint can look like distance
- That fear can look like indifference
- That love can exist without being felt
- That intention and impact are not the same

And most importantly:
That grief does not mean failure.

It means something that mattered.

Repairing a relationship between a stepparent and stepchild is not about forcing closeness or rewriting the past, it is about understanding what was possible, what was missed, and what may or may not still be safe to rebuild.

Sometimes healing means learning how to reconnect with patience, honesty, and boundaries. Other times, it means accepting that love existed, even if relationship could not. Neither choice is a failure.

Reconciliation requires willingness on both sides, but peace can be found even when paths remain separate. What matters most is releasing blame and honoring truth, the truth of what was given, what was needed, and what each person was capable of at the time.

**To the stepparent:**
Your love mattered, even if it was not fully seen.
Your restraint was not weakness.
Your presence had meaning, even if it was quiet.

**To the adult child:**
Your confusion does not make you ungrateful.
Your distance does not make you cruel.
You were responding to what you felt, not what was intended.

And sometimes, the most healing act is not repair, but understanding.

# Chapter 29

## How Unprocessed Trauma Shapes Parenting When Love Is Present

*How Unprocessed Trauma Shapes Parenting Even When Love Is Present......*

Most parents never intend to pass pain to their children.

They pass down what they learned to survive.

Not through cruelty.
Not through neglect.
But through patterns that once kept them emotionally alive.

This chapter is about the quiet ways trauma moves through generations, not because parents fail, but because unhealed experiences shape how emotion, closeness, and vulnerability are handled in the body.

And sometimes, the very things that helped a parent survive make it difficult for them to emotionally meet their child.

### Trauma Does Not Always Look Like Suffering

When people think of trauma, they often imagine something visible: abuse, abandonment, violence, or catastrophe.

But many parents carry a different kind of trauma, one that does not look dramatic but leaves lasting emotional imprints.

Trauma can also come from:

- Growing up in emotionally silent homes

- Being taught that feelings were weaknesses

- Having to mature too early

- Being parentified

- Living in chronic stress or instability

- Never being comforted when distressed

These experiences shape how the nervous system responds to emotion later in life.

And when those experiences are unprocessed, they do not disappear.
They become coping mechanisms.


## Why Some Parents Cannot Feel When Their Child Is Hurting

One of the most painful experiences for adult children is realizing that their parent did not respond emotionally when they were in distress.

Not because the parent did not care—but because the parent could not feel.

This emotional numbness is not indifference.
It is often **a trauma response.**

When a person grows up in an environment where emotions were unsafe, overwhelming, or ignored, the nervous system learns to shut them down in order to survive.

This is called **emotional blunting or emotional dissociation**

It develops when:

- Expressing feelings led to punishment or dismissal

- Emotions were ignored or minimized

- Crying was discouraged or mocked

- There was no safe adult to turn to

Over time, the body learns:
*Feeling is dangerous. Disconnect to survive.*

That disconnection can last decades.

## What This Looks Like in Parenting

When a parent with unresolved trauma becomes responsible for a child's emotional world, something difficult can happen.

They may:

- Freeze when their child cries

- Feel irritated or overwhelmed by emotional expression

- Shut down during emotional conversations

- Respond with logic instead of comfort

- Minimize pain without realizing it

- Become distant when emotions run high

Not because they don't love their child.

But because their nervous system never learned how to stay present with emotion safely.

To them, emotional intensity feels like threat.

## A Real-Life Example

A child falls and begins to cry not from injury, but from fear.

The parent reacts quickly:
"You're okay."
"Stop crying."
"You're fine."

From the outside, this looks like reassurance.

But inside the parent, something else is happening.

The child's distress activates the parent's own unresolved fear, helplessness, or emotional overwhelm from childhood.

The parent's body responds:
*This is too much. Make it stop.*

So they shut it down.

The child learns:
"My feelings make people uncomfortable."
"I should calm myself." "I
shouldn't need too much."

The parent believes:
"I'm teaching resilience."

The child learns:
"I'm alone with my feelings."

Neither intends harm.
But the emotional gap forms anyway. Why

## Parents Often Don't See the Damage

Parents remember what they did.
Children remember how it felt.

Parents remember:

- Working long hours

- Providing stability

- Protecting their children

- Making sacrifices

Children remember:

- Feeling alone when upset

- Not knowing where to bring their feelings

- Learning to be "easy"

- Feeling like emotions were inconvenient

This difference in memory is not denial.
It's perspective shaped by survival.

Parents were focused on endurance.
Children were focused on connection.

## When the Adult Child Grows Up

As the child becomes an adult, the emotional impact of this disconnection often becomes clearer.

They may notice:

- Difficulty expressing needs

- Fear of emotional dependence

- Feeling responsible for others' feelings

- Guilt when needing comfort

- A tendency to minimize their own pain

And when they become parents themselves, something shifts.

They suddenly feel:
"How could anyone ignore this?"
"How could a child's feelings be too much?"
"Why didn't I get this?"

This is not judgment.
It is clarity.

### What Parents Often Don't Realize

Many parents truly believe:
"I did the best I could."

And often, they did.

But doing your best does not mean nothing was missed.

A parent can:

- Love deeply

- Provide consistently

- Sacrifice greatly
  And still be emotionally unavailable.

Not because they didn't care.
But because they were never shown how.

### The Cost of Emotional Numbing

When emotional numbing goes unrecognized, it can lead to:

- Adult children who feel unseen

- Relationships built on performance, not safety

- Emotional distance that feels confusing to both sides

- Parents who feel rejected without understanding why

- Adult children who feel guilty for wanting more

Neither side is wrong.
Both are responding to inherited patterns.

## The Turning Point: Awareness Without Blame

Healing begins when parents can ask:
"What did I not know how to give?"

And when adult children can say:
"My parent's limits were not a reflection of my worth."

This is not about blame.
It is about honesty.

It is about recognizing that love alone does not heal trauma.
Presence does.
Attunement does.
Emotional safety does.

## What Breaks the Cycle

Cycles do not break through guilt.
They break through awareness.

When parents become willing to reflect instead of defend...
When adult children allow themselves to grieve without accusation...
When both sides recognize that trauma shaped behavior...

Something shifts.

Understanding replaces confusion.
Compassion replaces resentment.
And space opens for new ways of relating.

## A Closing Reflection

You can love deeply and still pass down wounds.
You can try your hardest and still miss what mattered most. You can be both caring and emotionally limited.

None of this makes someone a villain.

But awareness makes healing possible.

And healing when it begins does not just change one relationship.

It changes generations.

# Chapter 30

## What Healing Looks Like When the Past Cannot Be Changed

*Understanding Repair and the Work That Happens When Apologies Are Not Enough*

Healing does not require rewriting history.

It does not require perfect apologies.
It does not require reliving the past.
And it does not require proving who was right or wrong.

What it does require is something far more difficult:

**The willingness to acknowledge impact without defensiveness.**

This chapter is about what repair actually looks like when a parent realizes, often too late, that something in the emotional bond with their child was missing.

And it is also about helping adult children understand what meaningful repair looks like, so they no longer settle for partial accountability or emotional avoidance disguised as love.

### Repair Is Not the Same as Explanation

Many parents believe that explaining their circumstances should bring closure.

They say things like:

- "I was doing the best I could."
- "I had no support."
- "I was under a lot of pressure."
- "I didn't know any better."

These statements may be true.

But explanation is not repair.

Explanation focuses on the parent's experience.
Repair centers the child's emotional reality.

Repair begins when a parent can say, without defending themselves:

"I see how that affected you."
"I didn't realize you felt that alone."
"I can understand why that hurt."

Not:
"I didn't mean to."
"I did my best."
"You shouldn't feel that way."

The difference is subtle, but emotionally enormous.

**Why Accountability Feels So Threatening to**

**Parents**

For many parents, accountability feels like accusation.

Not because their child is attacking them, but because acknowledging emotional impact threatens their sense of identity.

If they admit harm, they fear:

- Being seen as a bad parent
- Having their sacrifices invalidated
- Losing their child's respect
- Being blamed for something they never intended

So instead of listening, they defend.
Instead of acknowledging, they explain.

Instead of staying present, they shut down.

This is not cruelty.
It is fear.

Fear that if they open the door to their child's pain, they will drown in guilt.

**Why Repair Matters More Than Intent**

Children do not heal from knowing their parent "meant well." They heal from feeling understood.

Repair requires:

- Listening without interrupting

- Allowing emotion without correcting it

- Acknowledging impact without self-protection

- Staying present when discomfort arises

Repair does **not** require:

- Perfect parenting

- Endless apologies

- Self-blame

- Agreeing with every detail of the child's experience

It requires **emotional humility**.

The ability to say:
"I see how this affected you, even if that wasn't my intention."
That sentence alone can repair years of distance.

**What Real Accountability Looks Like**

Healthy accountability sounds like:

- "I didn't realize how alone you felt."

- "I can see now that you needed more from me."

- "I wish I had known how to show up differently."

- "Your feelings make sense."

It does not sound like:

- "I guess I was a terrible parent then."

- "I did everything for you."

- "You're being unfair."

- "That was a long time ago."

Accountability is not self-punishment.
It is emotional presence.

## When Parents Cannot Offer Repair

This is one of the hardest truths in healing:

Some parents are not able to offer emotional repair.

Not because they don't care.
But because:

- They lack emotional insight

- They become overwhelmed by guilt

- They feel attacked by vulnerability

- They have never learned emotional language

Their own trauma remains unprocessed

This does not mean the child imagined the pain.
And it does not mean the parent is evil.

It means repair may have to happen without their participation.

**What Adult Children Must Learn**

One of the most painful lessons in adulthood is realizing:

Understanding does not always lead to change.

A parent may intellectually understand their child's pain and still be unable to respond emotionally.

This is where many adult children get stuck waiting for a moment that never comes.

Healing begins when the adult child asks:

- "What do I need in order to move forward?"

- "What kind of relationship is actually possible?"

- "What am I waiting for that may never happen?"

**Repair Can Be Internal**

When repair is not possible externally, it must happen internally.

This looks like:

- Validating your own experience

- Naming what you needed but didn't receive

- Letting go of the fantasy of emotional resolution

    Creating emotional safety elsewhere

- Releasing the need for acknowledgment to heal

This does not erase the relationship. It redefines it.

## What Healing Looks Like in Practice

Healing often looks quieter than people expect.

It looks like:

- Less arguing
- Less explaining
- Fewer emotional confrontations
- Clearer boundaries
- Lower expectations
- More peace

It looks like choosing emotional stability over emotional validation.

It looks like recognizing that love does not require emotional access.

## A Truth Both Sides Can Hold

Parents can love deeply and still cause emotional harm. Children can acknowledge pain without rejecting their parents. Both things can be true at once.

Healing happens when:

- Parents stop defending

- Children stop waiting

    Both stop trying to rewrite the past

- And start relating in the present with honesty

# Chapter 31:

## Learning to Live Without the Answer You Deserved
*Moving Forward When Closure Never Comes*

There comes a point in healing when the questions grow quieter, not because they have been answered, but because the cost of carrying them becomes too heavy.

Up to now, much of your emotional energy may have been organized around understanding:
Why did this happen?
What went wrong?
What could have been different?
Why wasn't I met the way I needed?

These questions were necessary. They helped you name what hurts. They gave shape to pain that once felt confusing and invisible.

But there is a stage in healing when understanding alone is no longer enough.

This is the stage where the nervous system begins to realize something difficult but clarifying:
Some answers may never come.
Some conversations may never happen.
Some people may never be able to give what you needed.

And healing must continue anyway.

## The Myth of Closure

Many survivors grow up believing that closure is something granted by another person.
An apology.

An explanation.

An acknowledgment.
A moment where everything finally makes sense.

But closure is not a transaction.
It is not something someone gives you once they understand your pain.

Psychologically, closure is an internal process. It happens when the nervous system stops organizing itself around waiting.

Waiting for insight.
Waiting for regret.
Waiting for emotional repair.

As long as healing depends on someone else's response, peace remains conditional.

This does not mean you stop caring.
It means you stop postponing your life.

**When the Search for Answers Keeps the Wound Open**

The mind often believes that if it can just understand *why*, the pain will soften.
But attachment pain does not live in logic. It lives in expectation.

A parent may explain their circumstances clearly.
They may acknowledge stress, pressure, fear, or lack of support
And still, something in you remains unsettled.

That is because explanation addresses *reason*, not *repair*.

A common scenario looks like this:

An adult child finally gathers the courage to talk to their parent

The parent listens.
They explain.

They say, "I didn't realize you felt that way."
They share how overwhelmed they were.

On the surface, it looks like progress.
But afterward, the adult child feels strangely empty.

Not relieved.
Not soothed.
Just... tired.

Because the nervous system was not seeking information.
It was seeking emotional presence.
And explanation cannot substitute for that.

When this happens repeatedly, continuing to seek answers can quietly keep the wound active.

Healing begins when you recognize that understanding does not always bring relief and stop asking it to.

It is redirection.

## What Letting Go Actually Looks Like

Letting go is often misunderstood.

It does not mean forgiving before you're ready.
It does not mean excusing harm.
It does not mean pretending the past didn't affect you.

Letting go means releasing the expectation that someone else must change in order for you to feel whole.

It looks like:

- No longer rehearsing conversations you'll never have

- No longer explaining yourself to people who can't hear you

- No longer placing your most vulnerable needs in the same places that couldn't hold them before

## Choosing Stability Over Resolution

There is a quiet shift that happens when healing takes root.

You begin to notice:

- You feel less reactive

- You ruminate less

- You don't feel the same urgency to be understood

- You stop measuring your worth by someone else's response

This is the nervous system settling.

You will choose to build your life around what's real."
This is emotional maturity.

## When Acceptance Becomes Freedom

Acceptance is often mistaken for defeat.
In reality, it is liberation.

Acceptance says:
"I see what is possible here and what is not."
"I will stop asking this relationship to become something it cannot be."
"I can honor what was missing without letting it consume me."

This is the moment when emotional energy returns to you.

You stop waiting.

You stop chasing.
You stop hoping that one more conversation will finally fix it.

And in that space, something else becomes possible:
Joy.
Stability.
Presence.
Choice.

## A Closing Truth

Healing does not always arrive with answers.
Sometimes it arrives with peace that no longer depends on them.

You are not weak for wanting understanding.
But you are strong when you decide your life does not have to pause without it.

Letting go of the answer you deserved is not giving up.
It is choosing to live.

# Chapter 32

## The Author's Letter to Her Daughters

To my daughters

I want to speak to you as your mother, clearly and honestly.

It was my responsibility to take care of your needs, not only to provide, protect, and guide you, but to be emotionally present, responsive, and able to recognize what you needed as a child. I understand now that this responsibility was mine. I see now that it was never your responsibility to adjust yourself to fit my limitations. I was the parent. It was my job to grow into the parent you needed.

There are things I see differently now.

I see moments when I was focused on surviving, managing, and doing what I believed was right, without fully understanding how my absence, my own childhood trauma, may have felt to you. Now I know that even though it was not my intention to hurt you, it doesn't erase how you were impacted. I also know that there were times when I did not show up in the way you needed me to show up as your mom.

If I could go back in time, I would celebrate your wins and comfort your losses. I would listen with more care. I would ask you how you were feeling instead of assuming you were fine. I would tell you more that I was proud of the person that you are right now, not the person that I wanted you to become. I would make space for your emotions, even when I felt overwhelmed or unsure how to respond. I would have trusted you more instead of believing that my way was always the correct way.

I cannot change the past, but I want you to know that I do not minimize it. I understand that parts of your experience may have been lonely, confusing, or painful, and that those feelings matter even if I did not recognize them at the time.

I am not asking you to forget what happened, excuse it. I am only asking for the opportunity to show up differently now.

If you allow it, I want to:

- Listen without defending myself
- Acknowledge your experience without correcting it
- Learn how to be emotionally present in ways I may not have known before
- Take responsibility through action, not just words My hope is not to erase the past, but to be accountable in the present.

I want you to know this:
What you needed mattered.
Your feelings were valid.
And it was my responsibility to see that. Always, remember that my love for you is endless and unconditional. There are no limits to it, no conditions attached. I am so proud of each of you of who you are, of how far you've come, and of all that you will become.

In ways you may never fully realize, your love has saved me. It gave me purpose, strength, and a reason to keep going when life felt heavy. You are my greatest gift and loving you has been the most meaningful part of my life.

With love and accountability,

Your Mom

Ingrid

## To My Reader Who Stayed

If you are reading this page, it means you stayed.
You walked through the hard parts.
You did not turn away when the truth felt heavy.

For that, I honor you.

God has brought you this far.
And He does not carry people this distance just to let them
fall.

The pain you've felt, the questions you've held, the love you've
tried to give even when it wasn't returned — none of it was
unseen. None of it was wasted.

Now something shifts.

It is time to begin learning the language your loved one speaks.
Not the words they say.
But the fears beneath them.
The silence.
The distance.
The way they learned to survive before they learned how to
connect.

This is not the end of your story.
It is the beginning of understanding.
And understanding is where healing finally has room to live.

You are still here.
That means there is still purpose.
Still growth.
Still love ahead.

And you will not walk the rest of this journey alone.

## Chapter 33

## An Invitation to Reflect and start the Healing Process

This work asks something simple, but not easy.

Ask yourself:

What did you lose after being separated from your parent?

Not what should have been lost.

Not what others think you should feel.

Not what looks like loss from the outside, but what you felt was missing on the inside.

Do not censor yourself.

Do not try to be fair, logical, or grateful.

Just be honest.

Go back as far as you can remember

_____

_____

_____

_____

_____

_____

_____

_____

_____

_____

For the following questions Keep in mind. You may notice small things at first:

- Someone not listening
- Comfort that didn't come
- Feeling alone in moments that mattered Or you may uncover deeper losses:
- A sense of safety
- Emotional closeness
- The freedom to need
- The feeling of being chosen There is no right or wrong answer.

This is not about blame.

It is about recognition.

What moments felt empty?

_____

_____

_____

_____

_____

_____

_____

_____

What did you need that didn't arrive?

_____

_____

_____

_____

_____

_____

_____

What changed without explanation?

_____

_____

_____

_____

_____

What did you need but stop asking for?

_____

_____

_____

_____

_____

_____

What did you learn to live without?

_____

_____

_____

_____

_____

_____

_____

Many people try to heal without ever naming what was lost. Bu
healing cannot begin in silence.

What remains unspoken often continues to shape us without
our awareness.

Naming loss is about finally giving it language.

This is the first stage of healing:

recognition.

## About the Author

I wrote this book from a place of reflection, lived experience, and a deep desire to understand myself more fully.

As a parent, I raised my children while carrying the weight of my own unresolved childhood trauma. Like many parents, I believed that love, stability, and good intentions were enough. I worked hard to provide for my children and protect them from the pain I once knew. What I didn't fully realize at the time was how unhealed experiences can quietly shape the way we show up as parents even when our children never complain.

As an educator, I approached my own healing the same way I approach learning: by asking questions, seeking understanding, and doing the research. I wanted to understand myself as a survivor of abandonment and how those experiences may have influenced my parenting, even in ways I never intended.

This book was born from that process. It is the result of reflection, study, and a desire to break patterns that often go unseen. Through this work, I came to understand that children can feel deeply affected even in loving homes, and that healing begins with awareness, not blame.

I wrote this book not only for myself, but for others who are searching for clarity, compassion, and understanding whether as parents, adult children, or both.

Because healing begins when we are willing to look honestly at our story and choose to grow from it

## Continue the Journey with The Awakening

If this book helped you recognize the wounds of abandonment, *The Awakening: Healing From Childhood Trauma and the Truth That a Child Cannot Stop Abuse* is the next step in your healing. This book gently guides readers into a deeper understanding of how childhood experiences shape emotional responses, relationships, and self-worth long into adulthood. It offers language for what many have felt but could never explain and clarity for what was never your fault.

*The Awakening* reminds you of a truth many carry in silence: a child does not have the power to stop abuse, change adults, or protect themselves from what they were never meant to endure. Healing begins when that responsibility is finally released.

If you are ready to understand your story with compassion instead of blame, and to begin rebuilding from a place of truth, this book will meet you there.

ISBN # 979-8-9930033-4-4